PRACTICAL LITERACY COACHING

A Collection of Tools to Support Your Work

JAN MILLER BURKINS

INTERNATIONAL
Reading Association
800 BARKSDALE ROAD, PO BOX 8139
NEWARK, DE 19714-8139, USA
www.reading.org

2455 TELLER ROAD
THOUSAND OAKS, CA 91362
www.corwinpress.com

CORWIN
A SAGE Company

The International Reading Association attempts, through its publications, to provide a forum
for a wide spectrum of opinions on reading. This policy permits divergent viewpoints without
implying the endorsement of the Association.

Executive Editor, Books   Corinne M. Mooney
Developmental Editor   Charlene M. Nichols
Developmental Editor   Tori Mello Bachman
Developmental Editor   Stacey L. Reid
Editorial Production Manager   Shannon T. Fortner
Design and Composition Manager   Anette Schuetz

Project Editors   Charlene M. Nichols and Rebecca A. Fetterolf

Cover   Design, Linda Steere; Illustration, © 2009 ImageZoo/Images.com, Inc.

Library of Congress Cataloging-in-Publication Data
Burkins, Jan Miller, 1968-
  Practical literacy coaching : a collection of tools to support your work / Jan Miller Burkins.
      p. cm.
  Includes bibliographical references and index.
  ISBN 978-0-87207-473-6
  1. Language arts teachers--In-service training--United States. 2. Language arts--United
States. 3. Reading--United States. I. Title.
  LB1576B8925 2009
  372.6--dc22
                                                                                                    2009009811
  Corwin Stock Number B74736P

For my mom

CONTENTS

ABOUT THE AUTHOR

Jan Miller Burkins is a full-time coach at Chase Street Elementary School, Athens, Georgia, USA. She has worked as a language arts consultant for a regional educational service agency, as a district-level literacy coordinator, as a reading specialist, and as an elementary classroom teacher. Her work as a consultant has taken her into elementary, middle, and high schools where she has helped school leaders examine their reading instruction, modeled lessons, and facilitated professional learning. Jan also is a part-time assistant professor at the University of Georgia where she teaches classes to students pursuing graduate degrees in literacy education.

In 1989, Jan received her undergraduate degree in early childhood education from Birmingham-Southern College in Birmingham, Alabama, USA, and in 1993 her master's from the University of Alabama. She later earned her reading specialist certification and her doctorate from the University of Kansas in 1999. Her dissertation, which was a meta-analysis of the research on phonemic awareness, was the Dissertation of the Year for the University of Kansas School of Education and one of three finalists for the International Reading Association's Dissertation of the Year.

Jan is the author of *Coaching for Balance: Meeting the Challenges of Literacy Coaching*. In addition to literacy coaching, Jan's professional interests include literacy in the content areas, using the visual arts to support literacy instruction, facilitating professional learning through inquiry, teaching for social justice, and the mechanics of guided reading and writer's workshop.

Jan lives with her husband, Nathaniel, and her four sons: 13-year-old twins Christopher and Duncan, 6-year-old Natie, and 1-year-old Victor. In her spare time, Jan takes pictures, writes poems, and practices the piano.

Author Information for Correspondence and Workshops
For consulting or workshop information or to share your explorations or variations of the tools in this book, contact Jan at janelizburk@aol.com.

My 5-year-old son lives in costume. Daily he finds accessories around the house that he imagines as part of some new persona: fireman, pilot, clown. The other morning as I was immersed in this work, Natie approached me requesting that I zip the part of his Spiderman costume that was beyond the reach of his little fingers. The subtle irony of his request struck me as funny; Spiderman needed his mother to zip up his suit before he could swing away on his web and save the world. Certainly, teachers are education's superheroes. In the present political climate, educators are responsible for more documentation, more instruction, more content knowledge, more professional learning hours, and more public scrutiny. While a teacher's list of responsibilities has always been amazingly long, it seems that of late it is almost endless.

Recently, some risk management advisors developed a Blood Born Pathogen Policy for a nearby school district. Administrators then distributed the policy among the teachers in the school system and directed them all to become familiar with it. A friend of mine who taught in this district dutifully studied it. This policy stated that teachers should, "Teach children how to stop their own bleeding." It further directed teachers to have the children practice this until they were proficient. So, along with new standards and curricula in traditional content areas, it seems that teachers must dust off their Boy Scout or Girl Scout first-aid training badges and teach their students to apply pressure to their wounds, as this is part of the many periphery curricula for which they are responsible.

In *Coaching for Balance: How to Meet the Challenges of Literacy Coaching* (Burkins, 2007), I maintain that literacy coaches, like teachers, are much like Superman and Wonder Woman. Read any literacy coach's job description and you are likely to agree; ours are jobs for superheroes. Furthermore, literacy coaching seems to be following a trajectory similar to that of classroom teachers; our lists of duties are exponentially expanding. Coaching positions that were initially held sacred have given way to myriad additional, and arguably unnecessary, responsibilities. With the novelty of coaching wearing thin, we become the extra pair of hands in the building. Given the trend toward misunderstanding our roles and given the enormity of the legitimate responsibilities we carry, it seems incumbent upon us to make every effort to share our work.

While you may not think of yourself as Superman or Wonder Woman, if you are juggling the many roles of a literacy coach, you are more like a superhero than you might think. You are probably leaping over tall bookrooms with a single bound, supporting change that is faster than a speeding bullet, and battling the evil forces that seek to take over the world of teaching through standardization of all kinds. So, with all you are doing to make the world of education a better place, let this book be the help you need to get the zipper on the back of your superwear zipped.

Sharing Our Work

Whenever I am with a group of coaches, I'm intrigued by the commonality of our concerns—not just our concerns but also our work. I have been struck by how helpful it has been to talk with other literacy coaching professionals about the very basics of how we engage in our varying practices. It seems that there are parallels and overlaps with the work we do with teachers, such that many of us are inventing and reinventing the same tools. It is this overlap that led me to publish this collection of tools and resources. Perhaps if we could claim some of this multiplicity of effort, we could be even more productive.

We are all creating observation forms; we are all creating rubrics for guided reading; we are all creating forms for documenting our time and for gathering feedback during professional learning. Perhaps this compilation of tools, which represents the diversity of tasks we perform with regularity, will prevent you from developing something that has already been created or give you a head start in developing a tool yourself. Please take the tools you find here and claim them for yourself. Utilize and vary them to suit your particular coaching context.

How This Book Came To Be

As previously mentioned, this book grew out of a realization that there is redundancy in our work that, if shared, could make all of our jobs a bit more productive. Once I proposed this book idea to the International Reading Association (IRA), I solicited submissions of tools through various literacy coach websites and simply through word of mouth. I also kept my ears and eyes open, and when I came in contact with a coach who had created something I thought might be valuable for other coaches, I requested permission to share it. I received more than 50 tools from literacy coaches and university professors all across the United States. In addition, I continued developing and piloting tools in my work. Coaches are an intelligent, creative lot, and I am thrilled to be able to illustrate that here. I narrowed and refined the collection of tools through my own work with them and with their developers, as well as through the peer review process for all publications submitted to IRA. Most important, as I scrutinized the various submissions, I returned to the assumptions and philosophies that I have tried to let shape and inform my literacy coaching practice.

Suppositions About Literacy Coaching

As a literacy coach, the heart of my work and the foundation of my practice has been the supposition that teachers are capable, dedicated, and caring. Furthermore, as I have read professional literature and as I have gathered tools, those that are rooted in these positive assumptions, and consequently in line with my coaching philosophy, are the ones that make the most sense for my work and my professional growth. Cathy Toll (2005) writes, "As long as there are millions of adults going to work every day at least in part because they care about children, we can hope for anything" (p. 135), and Donald McAndrew (2005) maintains that "Exemplary leaders believe that each stakeholder can be expected to perform well when the context encourages and supports that competence" (p. 20). Such assumptions that demonstrate hopefulness are the fuel of my work with teachers and are the common thread throughout the tools I included in this book. Throughout the process of writing and editing this text, I kept asking myself, What does the inclusion of this tool say about my beliefs about coaching? What will the subtext of my choice say to those who read it? The exercise proved enlightening for me, and I enjoyed the opportunity to reflect and revisit the beliefs to which I have worked to align my practice.

Toward the end of establishing more solidly for you my philosophical stance, I include the list of Assumptions of Goodwill that were originally printed in *Coaching for Balance* (Burkins, 2007, p. 78). These are the beliefs with which I try to align my actions. While I'm not always successful, I return to them again and again to realign my work with my established philosophy of coaching.

Assumptions of Goodwill

- Teachers want to be better at their jobs.
- Teachers want all of their students to be broadly literate.
- Teachers care about children.
- Teachers want to learn.
- Teachers want to teach.
- Teachers have the most difficult jobs in education.
- Teachers have the most important jobs in education.
- Teachers have the least respected jobs in a field that earns little respect.
- Teachers know the most about their children.
- Teachers want to be part of a larger learning community.
- Teachers are hard workers.
- Teachers are intelligent.

- Teachers are strong.
- Teachers are competent.
- Teachers want to do what is best for their students.
- Teachers want to know how to improve their instruction.
- Teachers can teach each other.
- Teachers have the right, the expertise, and the insight to play a critical role in decision making regarding curriculum, professional learning, assessment, and instruction.

From Philosophy to Action

While these tools were selected for inclusion in this book because they fit with the tenets I try to hold close in my work, it is easy for their intent to get lost in their interpretation. So, for purposes of further clarification, I want to share three guiding principles that I hope you will let influence the way you take these tools from the abstraction of the page to the realities of your school.

1. I don't keep notes on teachers that I would be uncomfortable sharing with them. The following question serves as my litmus test: How would I feel if I accidentally left these notes on the copier in the teacher workroom? In fact, all of the notes I make in classrooms—and this represents the bulk of my "documentation" about teachers—I copy for my files and give the original to teachers.

2. I don't use any kind of form in classrooms unless I have involved teachers in selecting, examining, or developing it. I do not walk into classrooms, make notes on an unexplained form, and then conference with teachers about how they did or did not meet the expectations set by that document.

3. This principle is related to the previous one; I do not use checklists in classrooms. I find that they are extremely limited, usually top-down, and rarely capture the many dimensions of a classroom. Most checklists, whether overtly or subtly, are supervisory tools.

Organization of This Book

This book is divided into six chapters. Each chapter opens with an introduction of Opening Thoughts to orient you to that group of tools. In addition to the section introductions, each tool (or sometimes cluster of tools) has a general description or orientation. If I did not develop the tool, the name of the developer(s) is included here, as well as suggestions for using it. In many cases, I include my rationale for selecting this tool for the collection as well as variations on its use.

My assignment of tools to chapters was, in many cases, a matter of considering the tool through one lens; however, a particular tool might have logically fit in a number of different sections. In the end, I found that most of the tools that made the final cut for inclusion passed a "versatility test." For example, a guided reading rubric could be used to support decisions about professional learning, as a self-assessment for teachers, or as a tool for gathering information while visiting classrooms. I believe the applications for these tools extend far beyond the limits of my suggestions and even beyond the limits of literacy coaching and into the realms of coaching across many content areas. Please don't limit your creativity in using these tools to the boundaries of my thinking. I encourage you to reach beyond the confines of my imagination.

The first chapter in this book, "Defining and Clarifying Your Role," includes tools fundamental to launching your literacy coaching work in ways that set you up for success. Chapter 1 explores the various aspects of your job, as defined by your school district. This section houses tools that can serve as the skeleton upon which you can hang your literacy coaching philosophy.

Chapter 2, "Stepping Into the Work of Literacy Coaching," is about communicating your role with the teachers in your school. This chapter maintains that the success of the coaching program you engage in is contingent upon teachers understanding the ways you can support them.

In Chapter 3, "Stretching Yourself," you will find tools for attending to your own professional learning. In this chapter I contend that in order for you to meet the demands of supporting the professional learning across an entire school you must be strategic in addressing your own needs for professional growth. The tools in this chapter are designed to help you stretch your own learning.

You will find resources for working with professional learning in Chapter 4, "Developing and Supporting Learning Communities." These tools are designed to help you support inquiry among teachers, manage the challenges of group work, and gather feedback from teachers. They are designed around the idea that the best professional learning is that which is designed to model the principles it is trying to teach.

Chapter 5, "Coaching Individual Teachers," is a collection of tools for recording what you see and hear in classrooms. It includes tools for supporting pre- and postobservation conferences with teachers and for encouraging teacher reflection. These tools are open-ended and designed to help you objectively capture classroom language. They are designed to support your visits to classrooms but are situated squarely on a philosophy that is respectful of teachers as the decision makers in their classrooms.

Because my philosophy of literacy coaching hinges on the presupposition of collegiality rather than supervision, you will see this thread running consistently through the forms in this chapter. These tools all align with a strengths-based perspective and are included here because they demonstrate positive assumptions of teachers.

Finally, Chapter 6, "Documenting Your Work, Managing Your Time," includes tools for recording the ways you spend your time. The purpose of this section is to increase the transparency of your work so that there aren't administrative impediments to your efforts to move forward. These tools are designed to make a record of your work without overloading you with documentation.

Finding the Right Tool

Within the structure described, there are other elements I have included to make it simpler for you to find the tool you need. My father is a dentist, and he impressed on me the importance of finding the perfect tool. I spent my high school summers working in his office. Occasionally a dentist somewhere would invent a new dental tool to accomplish some intricate dental procedure more efficiently, and my father would celebrate the ways this new tool would make his job more efficient. I can remember one particular time when he held some long metal instrument up and showed it to me. I don't remember exactly what procedure he was in the middle of, but I do remember him saying, "There is nothing like having the perfect tool." Whether the handle was made so that he could reach into the back of the mouth without getting in his own way or the working end was shaped exactly to fit between teeth 13 and 14, I can't remember. But I have always remembered what he said, and I have had the same experience in various coaching situations, particularly since I have begun working on this collection of tools.

To help you find the perfect tool for your particular coaching challenge and to make navigating the other various elements of this book straightforward, I have used a consistent and predictable organizational structure. First, each tool is sorted into the chapter topic most clearly related to its application. Second, the chapters are divided into the components that follow:

Coaching Connections—These are brief presentations of metaphors that have surfaced in my life outside of school and have informed the way I think about coaching. They represent the reflective overlap between my personal life and my professional life. Because coaching and mothering are the two biggest dimensions of my life right now, most of these anecdotes connect working in school with working with my family.

Coaching Stories—These are coaching vignettes, related directly to the topic of the chapter. I wrote these with the intent of offering you a coaching example that might provide insight into your own action. These are based on true stories of my work with teachers.

Related Research—In this section, I present research related to the tool or the topic of a particular section. These are brief summaries of sound research related to literacy coaching.

Tools—These are the specific forms, exercises, and protocols that are the heart of this text. In a number of instances, I include for your reference completed versions of the tools.

Links to *Coaching for Balance*—If you want to read more on a particular topic, these cross references will point you to correlated information in my previous book.

In addition, each chapter ends by asking you how you will apply this learning to your personal coaching context. The closing of each chapter offers a few resource recommendations that will support your further learning on the topic of the chapter, a few questions for reflection, and some possible action steps (although each of the forms in this book is basically an action step).

Conclusions: A Word About Imagination

The work of literacy coaches is in many ways a work of imagination. We imagine futures where student learning is rich and comprehensive. We imagine schools where all children have equal opportunities and access. We imagine educational systems that support rather than hinder teachers. We even imagine the best of teachers whose actions we might interpret as contrary to the positive assumptions we work to hold close.

Along these lines, Maxine Greene (1995) writes,

> I would suggest again, however, that it may well be the imaginative capacity that allows us also to experience empathy with different points of view, even with interests apparently at odds with ours. Imagination may be a new way of decentering ourselves, of breaking out of the confinements of privatism and self-regard into a space where we can come face to face with others and call out, "Here we are." (p. 31)

I encourage you to work imaginatively and to let the resources here spur you in this effort. Take this collection of tools, words, and ideas with you as you creatively and optimistically scale your literacy challenges like Spiderman on the tallest skyscraper. I hope you will find something here that will support you in your ongoing efforts to change the world.

ACKNOWLEDGMENTS

I f a writer writes acknowledgments, she is wise to keep them simple, to let "Thank you" elegantly bear the weight of gratitude. But a writer usually feels some obligation toward verbosity, so she will begin these efforts quite enthusiastically and matter-of-factly, thanking her editors, saying, for example, "Warmest thanks to Corinne Mooney and Charlene Nichols, my editors at the International Reading Association." Feeling writerly, she will elaborate, saying something like, "They capably organized my disorderliness and negotiated the tricky parts of revision with skill and honesty."

Having gained some momentum, she will move on, perhaps to all those who contributed work for inclusion in the book, for obviously she would not have a book to acknowledge at all without them. At this point she may feel a twinge of tenderness but will suppress it and press forward. She will acknowledge dear and generous colleagues, mentioning them by name, JoBeth Allen, Tom Cerbú, Krista Dean, Scott Ritchie, Claudia Taxel, Peggy Terrell, Kerstin Long, Brian Madej, who inspire and encourage her.

If she goes into any depth, perhaps referring to their kindness or intelligence, she may find the work of acknowledging growing difficult as that original twinge of tenderness resurfaces. She will use her mind to look into the faces one by one of those who have cared for her, and she will be profoundly moved. While she had grasped her sense of gratitude intellectually, the writer will find it surprisingly palpable when she sits still with the understanding that there are those who give to her consistently, who love her more ably than she loves them or even herself, and who want nothing in return for showing her how to care well.

This tangible sense of appreciation will present itself around the middle of writing the acknowledgements for her book. By then, in saying thank you in the front matter of a book, the writer will find that she is saying thank you for the whole of support that encompasses the life that surrounds the book. She will be startled to learn that acknowledging people is the kind of hard work that she is inclined to lean away from, because the very idea of it requires stepping beyond her sense of unworthiness.

She will look for alternatives at this point, back doors to gratitude. She will be inclined to write an acrostic poem with their names or lapse into lists, but she will avoid such lesser displays of appreciation. Rather full-flung, unbridled gratitude will be her only option. So she will shout out her "Thank yous" on the page, acknowledging her father, who thinks, even works at thinking, of ways to demonstrate support for her. "Where would I be without you, Daddy?" she will ask—and keep asking.

Then she will thank Daphne, who picks her up (literally) and brings her home (literally) and picks her up (metaphorically) and brings her home (metaphorically). To Daphne she will say, "Thank you for speaking truth and kindness, and for the violin lessons for the boy."

Finally, in a crescendo of gratefulness, she will try to acknowledge (even the word will sound trite to her) her husband, who is waiting at home for her when Daphne delivers her. He is waiting probably now with four children around him, perhaps the one boy has been practicing his violin. "You never doubted me for a minute," she will say to him, because he hasn't.

But it won't be enough for the writer, not any of it or all of it. And even after she has let her gratitude pool around her keyboard and her words keep piling up like disorderly stones to be arranged and rearranged, she will realize that they are completely inadequate anyway.

So the writer will simply say, "Thank you," which will be perfect for all these people who love her already.

Three Metaphors for Literacy Coaching

Conceptualizations are easier when we relate our efforts to mental maps, so I open this resource with three schematics related to literacy coaching that have developed through my conversations with coaches. In all of my professional efforts, I am surrounded, quite fortunately, by literacy and instructional coaches who are willing to engage in a continuous exchange of ideas. Brian Madej and Kerstin Long, instructional coaches in the district where I work, call the sparking of ideas that bounce from one person to the next "brain flint." So something one of us says will spark an idea in another's head. Thus has the social nature of learning dynamically contributed to the evolution of this book. So here for your own analysis, scrutiny, and professional conversation, I offer three literacy coaching metaphors that have sparked considerable exchange for us.

Metaphor 1: Coaching Pie

The first mental map or theoretical framework deals with the various ways a coach interacts with teachers (see Figure 1). Susan Bolen, another instructional coach in the Clarke County School District where I work, conceptualized this model. She thinks of our work with teachers as a "coaching pie," or a set of concentric circles, with the expanding layers representing the expanding professional learning groups. For example, the inner circle represents working with teachers individually. The next circle represents grade-level teams. The third circle represents working with study groups. Finally, the outer circle represents work that we do with the entire faculty. A particular teacher will have a "slice" of coaching that involves him or her at all the various levels of interaction.

As I reflect on Susan's model, I consider the ways it represents my present coaching work. I am collaborating closely with a handful of teachers, supporting them as they elevate their planning, watching their exchanges with students, and advising them on strategies for intervening

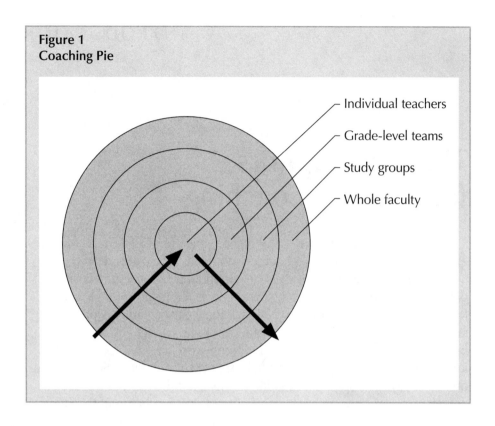

Figure 1
Coaching Pie

Individual teachers

Grade-level teams

Study groups

Whole faculty

with particular children. The beauty of this level of support is that it is inherently differentiated; I can adapt to the spontaneous needs of the teacher, which can prompt action and success.

I am also involved with a study group that meets weekly to examine the language we use with children. We are reading and responding to Peter Johnston's (2004) book *Choice Words: How Our Language Affects Children's Learning*. This is an optional study group, so all those in the group are highly motivated to honestly scrutinize the patterns of speech they use with children and with one another. The dynamics of a study group, particularly one that is shaped by participation choice, afford diversity of ideas without the limitations of a large group. There is texture without large-group dilution. Furthermore, any work with a learning community—whether study groups, grade-level teams, or vertical alignment teams within the larger learner community—promotes the development of both.

Finally, as illustrated by the outer circle of the diagram, I engage in learning events that enlist the entire faculty of my school in examining and expanding their praxis. Sometimes, these are brief events during our faculty meetings where I might present an instructional strategy on which we are all going to focus for a while or invite sharing of resources or experiences. Other times, the whole-faculty professional learning is extensive during an after-school session or on one of our professional learning days.

Brian, Kerstin, and I sat over lunch one day and talked about these concentric circles. We thought that, sometimes, the more intense work is up close, one on one, and that more general work is represented by the outer layer of the circles. However, at other times, the most significant learning for a teacher is initiated in a larger group setting. There have been times when I have facilitated professional learning with large groups that was deep and affected classroom instruction in surprising ways.

Basically, I think that the continuum of learning represented by these circles is bidirectional, depending on the teacher's needs at the time. With one teacher, a literacy coach may begin by working through whole-group sessions and moving toward one-on-one work. With others, literacy coaching work may be launched with individual support that establishes credibility with a teacher and leads to more valuable endeavors in small- and large-group contexts.

Metaphor 2: Nesting Dolls

The metaphor in this section illustrates the multiple levels of expertise that a coach must possess (see Figure 2). Scott Ritchie, a former instructional coach, and I (Burkins & Ritchie, 2007) experimented with a similar model as a way to illustrate how coaching represents multiple levels of content and pedagogical knowledge. This diagram developed around the idea of Russian nesting dolls or *matryoshka*, while simpler in general, still represents a very complicated hierarchy of expertise. First, literacy coaches are likely hired because they have skill in teaching children to read. They are usually proficient in working with and managing groups of children. Most often, their experience has spoken for them and heralded them as a likely candidate for a role in leading teachers in the area of literacy instruction. On a classroom level, literacy coaches have both content knowledge and the skill of implementation that makes this knowledge valuable. Second, represented by the relationship between the middle nesting doll and the outermost nesting doll, a literacy coach must have content knowledge about adult learning and be able to utilize this expertise through practical application to work with teachers.

A literacy coach must have all of this relational, experiential, and content expertise to influence classroom instruction. Skill in working with children without expertise in working with adult learners renders a literacy coach ineffective. Most of us know someone who was a great classroom teacher who later struggled with the differing demands of literacy coach or lead teacher. On the other hand, experience in supporting adult

Figure 2
Nesting Dolls Graphic

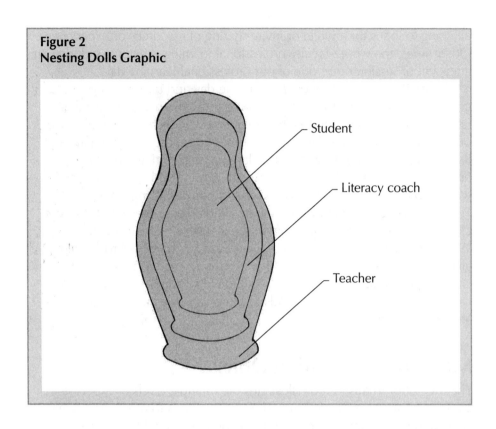

Student

Literacy coach

Teacher

learners without demonstrated skill in the classroom also compromises the credibility of the literacy coach.

This nesting doll metaphor describes the literacy coach's identity, a topic widely explored in coaching literature. Jennifer Allen (2006) asks, "Who am I? What am I? I have read all the definitions of reading coach, literacy specialist, and reading apprentice. I am reluctant to define myself as anything but a teacher" (p. 1). Jennifer's struggle with self-identifying as a teacher first is a common one among literacy coaches who, in fact, are teachers on at least two levels. Heather Hough and colleagues (2008) affirm this idea that "the work of coaching makes demands both on one's expertise in teaching children and on facility in working with other adults on improving their practice" (p. 9).

Even more complicated, reaching beyond the various levels of expertise and experience that a literacy coach might bring to a professional context, the demands of using this expertise in various roles are complex. Kristin Rainville and Stephanie Jones (2008) explain,

> The work of a coach involves far more than having a knowledge base in how teaching and learning work in literacy classrooms with children and

teachers. This complex work also involves deep understanding about situation enactments and how one's position will affect what happens in particular contexts. (p.447)

Furthermore, the struggle rests not only in literacy coaches negotiating the back and forth between their various banks of expertise but also in constantly asking themselves, "What support can you provide that will make the greatest difference in teaching?" (Rodgers & Rodgers, 2007, p. 123).

While this diagram is relatively simple, I think it represents what is one of the most complicated aspects of literacy coaching: "maintaining a 'historical' view across the relationships subsumed within the model" (Burkins & Ritchie, p. 6). Most important, literacy coaching requires that a coach move fluidly between these two levels, depending upon the demands of the coaching context. So the skill set is not categorical but more of a continuum, with the coach constantly moving back and forth along it.

Metaphor 3: Phases of the Moon

The third and final model I present here, again developed in collaboration with other coaches, is in reference to the Gradual Release of Responsibility (Pearson & Gallagher, 1983). The Gradual Release of Responsibility is represented most visibly in a coaching role through the application of coaching cycles (Lyons & Pinnell, 2001), which originated in the clinical supervision model (Goldhammer, 1969). The Gradual Release of Responsibility involves the coach first demonstrating an instructional strategy, then practicing with the teacher in ways that gradually give the teacher more and more responsibility, and finally watching the teacher as he or she implements the newly learned strategy alone. This release of responsibility provides security for teachers and allows coaches to catch implementation mistakes before they are habituated. Furthermore, because it is cyclical, teachers become involved in professional learning processes that support their ongoing development; this work is not periodic but continual.

Recently, I facilitated a professional learning event with a group of coaches who developed a model that illustrates this sharing and releasing of responsibility. This group of coaches from Hall County School District in Georgia includes Darlene Doster, Debbie Bagwell, Shelley Collier, and Pat Barrett. They represented the stages of the Gradual Release of Responsibility by drawing the phases of the moon (see Figure 3).

With a new moon, the teacher is not reflected in the work but is simply observing the coach as he or she demonstrates a new instructional

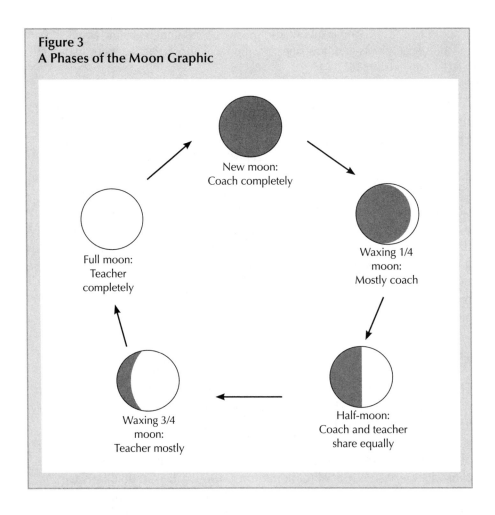

Figure 3
A Phases of the Moon Graphic

New moon:
Coach completely

Waxing 1/4
moon:
Mostly coach

Full moon:
Teacher
completely

Half-moon:
Coach and teacher
share equally

Waxing 3/4
moon:
Teacher mostly

method. At the second phase of the moon, the teacher is beginning to have a presence in the work and is represented by the waxing moon. The literacy coach is still doing the heavy lifting at this point, but the classroom teacher is also carrying some of the weight. At the third phase of the moon, the classroom teacher and the literacy coach are sharing responsibility equally; thus, the teacher is represented by the half-moon. With the fourth phase of the moon, the teacher is engaged in the bulk of the work and the literacy coach is less present. This is represented with the moon at three quarters. Finally, the literacy coach is no longer present as the classroom teacher is represented in a full phase. The completion of this cycle, of course, marks the beginning of another, as the literacy coach might engage in demonstrating something new. Thus, while this model may not hold up to intense scientific examination, I think it represents the cyclical nature of coaching and the waning role of the literacy coach in supporting teachers in broadening their pedagogy.

Closing Thoughts: Using Metaphors in Coaching Conversations

I love getting together with coaches and saying, "What do think about this model, metaphor, or map as a way to describe our work?" With all the conversations in which I have participated and with all the texts on literacy coaching I have explored, I have yet to come across a model that is comprehensive or specific enough to encompass the many aspects of literacy coaching.

Perhaps these mental maps would not hold up under the scrutiny of a coaching cartographer, but they are, rather, for you to consider generally rather than precisely. They are simple metaphors used to examine very complex systems. They are most valuable, I think, as conversation pieces, explored as part of a collection of ways to talk about and understand our work. So I put forth these three in combination and as a place for you to begin developing mental maps of the various aspects of your literacy coaching work. Once again, I invite you to develop your own or expand on these.

CHAPTER 1

Defining and Clarifying Your Role

"The more we allow ourselves to unfold, the less likely we are to unravel."
Irwin Kula

Opening Thoughts: Finding Ourselves

I recently collected from my mailbox six books about literacy coaching that I am previewing for a spring course. Of the six, five open with chapters that are basically "What is a literacy coach?" (cf. Jay & Strong, 2008; McKenna & Walpole, 2008; Moran, 2007; Mraz, Algozzine, & Kissel, 2009; Sandvold & Baxter, 2008). This is not surprising considering the confusion under which many coaches work.

In 2007, I attended the International Reading Association (IRA) convention in Atlanta, Georgia, USA. During this conference, hoards of literacy coaches made their way to Atlanta to learn more about literacy and about coaching. While there, I tried to initiate conversations with as many coaches as possible and learn about the work we are doing. It seems that there are as many literacy coaching contexts as there are coaches. Surprisingly, it is not uncommon for the administrators who are hiring a literacy coach to have little idea what a coach should do, and, in many cases, the literacy coaches are mired in confusion as well. In some cases, principals are simply assigned a coach, with little explanation of how the coach might support teachers or how the administrator might support the coach. To muddy things further, many coaches can trace this confusion all the way up the chain of command. This is leading to some tenacious misunderstandings in the field and introduces the risk of diluting the impact of literacy coaching (IRA, 2004).

The tools that follow are designed to help you define and clarify the work in which you are engaging in schools, both for yourself and for those you work with and for. The aim of this effort is to help you focus your energy and to establish a coaching vocabulary between you and your administrators and you and your teachers.

Needless to say, not all coaching positions are created the same and some positions described as "coaching" have little to do with the work of supporting teachers as they improve their instructional practice. My hope is that the tools in this section will inform the decision making of literacy coaches and administrators as they are crafting their job descriptions, establishing the boundaries of their work with teachers, and devising ways to gauge the effectiveness of the coach. Perhaps some of these tools will serve to help administrators and literacy coaches launch literacy coaching in their schools in ways that influence the productivity of their work and the longevity of their roles. While so many principals and literacy coaches are struggling to establish coaching programs and are arriving at approximations that are expensive in terms of relationships with teachers and energy of coaches, here is a concrete place to start exploring what to do and what not to do so that you can engage in less trial and error and in more thoughtful decision making.

If you have already defined and initiated your coaching role in a school and you are rethinking your approach, it is not too late to redefine yourself. These tools hold merit for both the novice and the experienced coach seeking to consider the ways he or she approaches the work of coaching.

Coaching Connection: Living Horizontal in a Vertical World

Thoughtful decision making in the early days of a literacy coaching position is critical because such decisions set in motion patterns of work that may be challenging—although not impossible—to change later. In the earliest work of coaching, it is essential for a literacy coach to pause and reflect before acting. Coaches who are not proactive in developing their roles at the onset of their jobs are likely to find themselves stepping into responsibilities that are incongruous with what they believe about teaching, learning, and literacy coaching.

The other night my 6-month-old son was lying in his playpen. He was on his back, babbling to the rest of the family and looking around the room very seriously. My husband commented that he lives horizontal in a vertical world, and his comment gave me pause. How must it be to exist in a world where your perspective is always different from everyone else's? Literacy coaches who have fallen into coaching roles accidentally rather than strategically may find themselves in this situation. Even when literacy coaches are thoughtful about establishing the parameters of their jobs, maintaining these limits can remain a continuous challenge.

In fact, for literacy coaches, negotiating the difference in our vantage point and that of others around us is our daily exercise. Whether we are coaches under pressure to act as administrators or constructivists trying to exist in a standardized universe, the analogy of horizontal and vertical worlds meshing is applicable for many of us.

Related Research: Four Schools, Three Literacy Coaches, and 160 Teachers

Donna Johnson-Lambert (2008), a literacy coach and friend of mine, conducted a fascinating case study that demonstrated how different views of coaching can exist in a school. She examined how four schools representing the primary, elementary, middle, and high school grades within one school system have defined the role of literacy coach. Johnson-Lambert included the county superintendent, the principals from each school, the literacy coaches from each school, and a select group of teachers representing different years of experience and a range of grade levels. She interviewed the superintendent, principals, some teachers, and coaches, and she gave the teachers surveys to complete.

Johnson-Lambert found that what the administrators, teachers, and coaches saw as the role of the literacy coach differed greatly. In addition, administrators and coaches were likely to espouse a philosophical stance and then act in ways that were incongruous. For example, one administrator expressed a strong sentiment that the primary work of the literacy coach was with teachers and in classrooms. However, in reality, the same administrator frequently asked the literacy coach to take on additional responsibilities and to attend meetings and trainings off campus. Interestingly, the coach's absence was noted by teachers who completed Johnson-Lambert's survey.

Johnson-Lambert writes,

> Through the collection of this data, as well as from additional research, this researcher has concluded that the role of a literacy coach may be defined by a system and assumed by the administration, but if it is not clearly presented to the teachers and created around their specific needs, the role of literacy coach cannot truly be felt within the school system. (p.3)

The lesson from Johnson-Lambert's research is that literacy coaches and administrators must decide from the onset the nature of the literacy coach's work within the school and then must act in ways that are aligned to these early decisions.

Tools for Defining and Clarifying Your Role

Orientation to Tool 1: Literacy Coaching Role Reflection Guide

Whether you are exploring the possibility of becoming a literacy coach or you are a seasoned literacy coach committed to reflective practice, the tool below will give you an opportunity to focus your thoughts. The following worksheet, developed by Douglas Fisher and his colleagues at San Diego State University, San Diego, CA, USA—Nancy Farnan, Leif Fearn, Diane Lapp, and Nancy Frey—is a tool to help you to think deeply about the current direction in your work as a literacy coach.

I see at least three uses for this tool. First, if you are already a literacy coach, this preparatory worksheet can help you think about the school year ahead. One of the lovely things about education is that every year gives us a clean start. We have a few weeks of summer to reinvigorate and renew and then we get to refocus our energies with a fresh perspective. My suggestion to experienced literacy coaches is to adapt this worksheet and consider your responses to the questions listed. Use the exercise to reexamine your beliefs and reflect on your experiences relative to a new school year. I completed this form in preparation for this book and found that it informed my work even after six years of coaching. In thinking back across my years as a coach, I would have completed this form differently at the onset of each school year. Thus, as a series of historical documents it would have captured my learning and professional growth over time.

As a novice coach, use this tool as a way to set in motion a literacy coaching initiative that is rooted in clarity of purpose. Take the time that reflection requires in order to set yourself and the teachers in your building up for success. This initial investment promises great dividends in relationships with teachers and instructional improvement.

As a new or prospective literacy coach, you can use this reflective tool in preparation for a job interview or to consider the challenges and the joys of the work. Weigh carefully whether this field is a fit for you. Such an exercise can support you in considering your beliefs and philosophy of coaching so that you don't find yourself accepting a job that does not allow you to coach in ways that are aligned with your belief system.

LINK TO COACHING FOR BALANCE

To read more about aligning your coaching beliefs to your work, see "Defining Our Beliefs About Literacy Coaching" on page 15 in Chapter 1.

LITERACY COACHING ROLE
REFLECTION GUIDE

Name _____ Date_____

Questions	Reflections
1. How have your experiences and training prepared you to perform the particular duties and responsibilities of the literacy coach that are most pressing for your school?	
2. How have your experiences facilitating professional learning influenced the way you will develop and support a culture of learning in the school?	
3. If you were facilitating professional learning during the first weeks of school, what topic would you choose? Why? What might a participant expect in the professional learning experience?	
4. Describe the role of performance standards and curriculum in driving instruction. How will you support teachers in using performance standards and the district curriculum to make instructional decisions?	
5. What professional development activities (readings, conferences, peer coaching) have you recently experienced, and what did you learn from them? How will they influence your understandings and practice?	
6. What do you think are the primary roles of a literacy coach? How will you communicate and develop these roles with teachers?	
7. What about literacy coaching excites and concerns you?	

Created by Douglas Fisher and colleagues at San Diego State University.

Orientation to Tool 2: Questions for Interviewers Rubric

While the Literacy Coaching Role Reflection Guide can help you consider what you might say in an interview for a literacy coach position or how you will move forward in a new year, the Questions for Interviewers Rubric is designed to help you think about the questions you might ask in an interview. Furthermore, it gives you some sample responses that can help you gauge the alignment of the position to the authentic spirit of literacy coaching.

The rubric that follows was developed by the 2007 Literacy Coach Cohort from the University of Georgia, USA. This cohort includes Lois Alexander, Leslie Barrett-Jones, Tonia Bowden-Paramore, Molly Kendrick, Susan Kiningham, Darcie St. Onge, Sharon Smith, Ann Tweedell, and Michelle Vechio-Weinmeister. They wanted something to support them as they pursued literacy coaching positions in schools. They understand that all literacy coaching positions are not equal and that misconceptions about coaching abound. The cohort developed this rubric to make sure that they were pursuing positions that supported their philosophy of coaching and that would set them up for success.

However, in reality, there aren't many dream jobs. Sandvold and Baxter (2008) write,

> Any coaching plan should be flexible so that it may be adjusted for changing demands or issues that haven't been considered—after all, no matter how well you do your homework, you won't think of everything! Of course, you want to get as much right from the beginning as possible. (p. 7)

When I examine this rubric, there are parts of it that describe my job as authentically aligned to coaching in its truest sense, and there are other places where the rubric illustrates some of the challenges I face. I think that most literacy coaching jobs are dreamy in some areas and challenging or out-of-sync in other areas. However, it is worthwhile to enter a position understanding the negotiations in which you will need to engage if you are going to maintain your core beliefs. The point of the rubric is not to present you with a model of coaching that is so ideal it can exist only in theory but to help you stay balanced, thoughtful, and proactive.

QUESTIONS FOR INTERVIEWERS RUBRIC

Run! Don't take this job no matter how much they want to pay you.	This could work out. There is definitely room for improvement, but there is a foundation here upon which you can build.	This could be your dream job. Sign now!
What is your primary goal in hiring a literacy coach?		
We decided to hire a literacy coach because we have many teachers who don't understand how to teach reading and we really need someone to come in and fix them. In addition, we have very low test scores and many of our students are in need of remediation. However, you must remember that this is a temporary position and will not be funded unless we see dramatic improvement in our students' scores.	We have very low test scores and very high ESL and special education populations. Therefore, we have chosen to implement the new "No Reader Left Behind" program. By hiring a literacy coach, not only will we have someone to help educate our teachers about this program but also we will have someone to assist with its numerous assessments and remediation procedures.	A committee of teachers, parents, and administrators identified literacy as a primary concern for our students. They proceeded to explore a variety of options that would help to alleviate this problem and were all very enthusiastic about their findings regarding the use of a literacy coach. After presenting this idea to the remainder of the faculty, it became evident that a literacy coach could play an essential role in helping us meet our literacy goals.
What do you see as my three top priorities as a literacy coach?		
1. Implementing our new basal reading program. 2. Increasing our test scores. 3. Reporting to the administrator what the teachers are doing wrong in their classrooms.	1. Helping teachers who may need support in their reading and writing instruction. 2. Planning professional learning to meet goals we have already identified. 3. Analyzing assessment data and using the data to improve test scores.	1. Planning effective professional learning based on the needs of the teachers and supporting the development of professional learning communities. 2. Working with individual teachers to improve student achievement on many measures of achievement 3. Fostering a collective love of reading and writing across the school community (including teachers, students, parents, and community members).

(continued)

Practical Literacy Coaching: A Collection of Tools to Support Your Work by Jan Miller Burkins.
© 2009 International Reading Association. May be copied for classroom use.

Run! Don't take this job no matter how much they want to pay you.	This could work out. There is definitely room for improvement, but there is a foundation here upon which you can build.	This could be your dream job. Sign now!
What do you and your faculty see as my primary role in your school?		
As you know we are in definite need of improvement in the area of language arts. We feel certain that with your knowledge and background you can "fix us" and implement the programs that the district is suggesting we use.	The concept of a literacy coach is new to us, but one that we are very interested in. We know that we would like you to be our literacy leader and help guide our teachers in the areas of best practices in reading and writing instruction. However, we value your input in regards to what your duties and responsibilities would be.	We see your primary role as literacy leader. We would look to you to support teachers in professional development, conduct non-evaluative classroom observations, and provide feedback to support teachers as they implement strategies that they are learning. Your position would have additional responsibilities, but we are open to negotiating these with you and value your input in crafting your job description.
What is your understanding of a productive relationship between a literacy coach and a principal?		
You will need to report frequently to the principal, because you'll be in the classrooms and see what the teachers are actually doing. You will take orders from both the principal and assistant principal. You will need to check in with them daily to see where you may need to fill in.	You will be considered one of the administrative staff, but you will need to work well with teachers. We may ask you to make periodic reports concerning your work with language arts teachers. This report would include any particular problems you encounter in your observations.	We expect you to work well with both the administrators and the teachers. You will be part of the decision-making team, particularly in adoption of programs relating to reading and language arts, but you will not have an evaluative role. You will often be asked to participate in the hiring process of new teachers. You will be expected to relate any serious problems you see as you visit classrooms.

(continued)

Run! Don't take this job no matter how much they want to pay you.	This could work out. There is definitely room for improvement, but there is a foundation here upon which you can build.	This could be your dream job. Sign now!
What have you told your teachers about this position?		
Nothing; our superintendent just told us that we had to hire a literacy coach.	Money has just been appropriated for this position, so the faculty does not know that we are hiring, but this is a request that has come up in discussions about improvement. We want the person we hire to help us explain the role of the coach to the faculty.	You met a few of the teachers you'll be working with because they are here on the interviewing committee. We've had several faculty meetings developing an improvement plan. This position is a request from our teachers, after several different options. A committee visited schools with literacy coaches and conducted interviews with working literacy coaches and teachers. Teachers have had a great deal of input into the role of a literacy coach in our school.
What will be my role in assessment?		
You will be responsible for designing or locating the best assessments to use with our students. You will also be responsible for completing all assessments, recording the data, and suggesting teaching strategies to teachers based on the assessment results.	We have a need to use assessments that will accurately reflect the literacy competency of our students. We do not have a consistent practice in place at this time for assessments. You will need to locate assessments, organize test materials, and train the teachers in the best way to use assessments. There will also be times you will be responsible for tracking student data. You may also need to help give assessments at times, but it will not be the bulk of your job.	We have been working very hard to use effective assessment practices at our school. We use a variety of assessments in addition to data from standardized tests. You will be responsible for using data to inform the coaching you are doing. You will also be expected to look for additional assessments that may better inform our work and provide training in these. It is important for the teachers to assess their children to get a feel for where they are, but there may be times you are asked to help administer assessments as a way of training teachers.

(continued)

Run! Don't take this job no matter how much they want to pay you.	This could work out. There is definitely room for improvement, but there is a foundation here upon which you can build.	This could be your dream job. Sign now!
How would you like me to handle a situation in which a teacher is not being successful and may need more intervention than I can provide?		
If you ever have a problem with a teacher, you need to inform me so that I can get with him/her and solve the problem. Or More intervention than you can provide? It may be that you will then need to team teach with the teacher until he/she can again gain control. This is your area of expertise, isn't it?	I would like for you to inform me when a situation like this occurs. I would like to discuss what interventions you have tried before I get involved. I will go from there to decide what steps to take next.	Please document all forms of intervention strategies you use to help the teacher. We can get together and brainstorm more possible interventions. I don't want the teacher to feel like a failure, but I don't want the problem to go on. I also don't want to break the trust I know you will have built with the teacher. It may require that I schedule more observations. We'll handle this together if this problem should arise, and I won't move on an issue without meeting with you so that I won't compromise your future work with other teachers.
How do you plan to maintain the boundaries of a literacy coach as a support person rather than an administrator?		
Well, we're going to need to talk about that. How strongly do you feel on this issue? I'm going to need you to enforce the expectations we're putting out there and let me know when and who isn't keeping up with their end of the deal. That's just par for the course with this job.	I didn't realize that was going to be a major issue. Can you explain to me a little why this is such a strong variable in your success as a coach? I'm not saying I won't support this consideration, just that I need some basis and understanding for recognizing its importance.	I completely understand how necessary it is for you to be in a nonthreatening position with faculty. Anything I can do to support development and help preserve those relationships, you just let me know. Rest assured I won't ask you to do anything that I or you believe may jeopardize these boundaries.

(continued)

TOOL 2

Run! Don't take this job no matter how much they want to pay you.	This could work out. There is definitely room for improvement, but there is a foundation here upon which you can build.	This could be your dream job. Sign now!
How much time will be allotted for (a) my professional development and (b) working in professional development groups with teachers?		
We are hiring you because we feel that you already have a strong knowledge base in the area of literacy coaching. In order for you to facilitate change, we need you here and, therefore, do not feel compelled to grant you release time during the school day to explore professional development. We feel like this can be accomplished outside of school hours. As far as working in professional development groups with teachers, we don't see this as your main focus. We need you to spend as much time in classrooms modeling instruction, observing, providing feedback, and interacting with students as much as possible.	This is certainly open for discussion, and I would welcome your input. While I feel like you are highly qualified, I understand the importance of ongoing professional development. Perhaps you could submit a proposal outlining your professional development needs. Additionally, I can see the value of you working in professional development groups with teachers, and this is an area for which I would like you to assume responsibility. However, I am not sure how much time this really requires and feel like I need an idea of the goals that the teachers wish to accomplish.	Professional development is highly regarded at this school as we understand the value of continuing to nurture your own professional knowledge. I feel certain that we can strike a balance between your duties as a facilitator and your needs as a learner. All I ask is that you submit a professional development plan to me that outlines the activities and amount of time that you need. Together we can review this and come up with a plan that will ultimately be mutually beneficial to us both. In regards to professional development with teachers, I believe ongoing, well-thought-out development is necessary for any change to occur. I am certainly open to hearing your ideas and the time requirements that you feel are necessary to effectively implement change.

Created by Lois Alexander, Leslie Barrett-Jones, Tonia Bowden-Paramore, Molly Kendrick, Susan Kiningham, Darcie St. Onge, Sharon Smith, Ann Tweedell, and Michelle Vechio-Weinmeister.

Practical Literacy Coaching: A Collection of Tools to Support Your Work by Jan Miller Burkins.
© 2009 International Reading Association. May be copied for classroom use.

Orientation to Tool 3: Literacy Coach Job Description Worksheet

As described previously, it is common for districts to hire educators to fill literacy coach positions when the district really does not understand the work of a literacy coach. Cathy Toll (2008) writes,

> the success of literacy coaches is impeded by a variety of factors: competing programs of instruction; questionable understanding of the literacy process among educational leaders, policy makers, and teachers; failure to clearly define the role of literacy coaches; lack of attention to characteristics of adult learners; and so on. Still we go to work every day with hopes for the success of literacy coaching. (p. 10)

Many literacy coaches are in positions where they are crafting their job descriptions on the run as they are initiating their work with teachers. In such cases, it is to the benefit of the coach and the school for the literacy coach to be proactive in establishing the definitions of his or her work. In other words, if this is your situation, don't wait for someone to come and tell you what to do, because you will run the risk of your school's leadership giving you responsibilities that don't align with your philosophy of literacy coaching. If you are in the position of crafting your own job description, consider yourself fortunate and get busy.

I developed this worksheet after I examined a collection of literacy coach job descriptions from districts around the U.S. This process was enlightening. If I ever had any misunderstandings about the depth and breadth of literacy coach work, they were clarified for me through this exercise. With some very informal analysis, patterns emerged. Most literacy coach job descriptions I studied included items defining work in eight different areas: character, culture, expertise, vision, assessment and data analysis, professional learning, work in classrooms, and program implementation. The categories are condensed below to present a reflective tool for literacy coaches who are involved with defining their own roles. For each category, there is space for development—that is, space for a coach to process and brainstorm or even fine-tune a job description.

I have completed this tool from the perspective of a practicing literacy coach, and I have also found it helpful to reflect on the responsibilities I already carry in my school. This tool gives experienced coaches the opportunity to scrutinize the language of literacy coaching and set themselves up for success. For example, what are the implications of "supporting" and "assisting" versus "monitoring"? If a job description says, "Implements a schoolwide assessment system for monitoring student achievement," a coach may wonder who will intervene with teachers if the data indicates there are problems.

LINK TO COACHING FOR BALANCE

To learn more about what literacy coaches do, read "What Is a Literacy Coach?" on page 28 in Chapter 2.

LITERACY COACH JOB DESCRIPTION WORKSHEET

Coach_____ Date_____

Area 1: Character—What personality traits does a coach need to be successful?
(Ex: Listens well, has strong work ethic, demonstrates flexibility, etc.)

Development:

Area 2: Culture—What are the ways of working and learning together that a coach should help establish?
(Ex: Establishes stance of continual learning, promotes tenets of social justice, develops learning communities, fosters culture of trust, etc.)

Development:

Area 3: Expertise—What content knowledge and skill must a coach possess?
(Ex: Understands the reading process, demonstrates skill in effective classroom practices, holds expertise in reading research, can establish credibility with teachers, etc.)

Development:

Area 4: Vision—What leadership skills must a coach possess?
(Ex: Communicates a sound literacy vision for school, understands steps required to reach literacy goals, develops short- and long-term plans, etc.)

Development:

(continued)

Area 5: Assessment & Data Analysis—How should data inform the work of a literacy coach? (Ex: Exhibits comfort and skill with data analysis, uses data to shape classroom practice, collects data and reflects on the progress of students, etc.)
Development:
Area 6: Professional Learning—How should a coach contribute to the professional learning of teachers? (Ex: Facilitates study groups, provides schoolwide professional learning, inventories professional learning needs of teachers, etc.)
Development:
Area 7: Work in Classrooms—How should a coach support the professional learning of teachers within the classroom context? (Ex: Scaffolds teacher professional learning through demonstration lessons, watches teachers teach and supports their reflection, supports teacher learning through a gradual release model, etc.)
Development:
Area 8: Program Implementation—What is the role of the coach in supporting the implementation of the established reading program? (Ex: Coordinates the implementation of the school reading program, distributes literacy program materials, facilitates management of the bookroom, evaluates and helps select reading materials, etc.)
Development:

Orientation to Tool 4: Literacy Coach Evaluation Form

If the job descriptions of literacy coaches are vague, then it follows that the evaluation of coaches is often nonspecific. It is in the best interest of the coach to investigate upfront, and establish if necessary, the design of his or her evaluation. This tool is one example of a form used in the evaluation of a literacy coach. It was developed by Mark Tavernier for the Clarke County School District in Athens, Georgia, USA, where I work. Clarke County has taken great care to make sure that the job descriptions of literacy and instructional coaches are clear and in alignment with the district goals. They have made sure that the accompanying evaluation forms are parallel with those job descriptions.

If at all possible, I would suggest being proactive in identifying or developing the tool with which your performance will be documented. If your school or district has already developed an evaluation instrument or process for your work, make understanding it one of your first priorities as a literacy coach. You do not want to receive this information at the end of the year, when your practice all year may have been based on different information or none at all.

I have a copy of my job description hanging in my office. This display makes it easy for me to revisit the elements on which my administrators will evaluate me and to keep my practice aligned with the responsibilities I was hired to execute. While this may seem inhibiting, I actually find it relieves pressure. As a literacy coach, having complete information about the expectations for your role will actually make it easier to operate successfully within your job description. If you find the elements of your evaluation confining, then perhaps the coaching position in which you have found yourself does not align with what you believe to be important for the work of a literacy coach.

LITERACY COACH EVALUATION FORM

Coach _____ School _____

Preconference _____ Final conference _____

Quarter 1 date _____ Quarter 2 date _____ Quarter 3 date _____

4 = Fully developed   3 = Evidence   2 = Some/limited evidence   1 = No evidence

	4	3	2	1
Provides instructional support for teachers				
Models lessons in classrooms				
Provides multiple classroom coaching experiences for individual teachers to assist with the implementation of curriculum/instructional practices				
Models routines, procedures, and rituals				
Models the use of technology as an instructional tool				
Arranges for peer observations in other classrooms				
Assesses student progress				
Assists teachers in creating and using assessments and tasks that align to the district curriculum				
Assists teachers in examining student work to share and compare scoring of classroom-based assessments				
Guides and assists teachers in using formative assessment results to continuously monitor, assess, and evaluate student progress				
Guides and assists teachers in using formative assessment results to modify classroom instruction				
Collaborates with administration and staff				
Provides training on the use of district curriculum guides and related instructional materials and resources				
Plans with and guides teachers as they sequence and organize instruction				
Supports professional learning in a variety of ways (coaching, collaborative planning, demonstration and modeling, dialogue, discussion, study groups, etc.)				
Establishes regular times to meet with the administration to discuss progress				
Communicates, in person, with the administration in a timely manner				
Participates in ongoing training and support sessions for instructional coaches				
Comments:				

Created by Mark Tavernier.

Practical Literacy Coaching: A Collection of Tools to Support Your Work by Jan Miller Burkins.
© 2009 International Reading Association. May be copied for classroom use.

A Coaching Story: Crossing Lines

The value of examining your job description thoroughly and taking the care to weigh it against your personal and professional belief systems is that, in doing so, you set in place boundaries that will guide your daily practice as a literacy coach. These are the lines with which you are likely to wrestle, or to even find yourself inadvertently crossing at times. Nevertheless, they are a place to which you can return when you catch yourself compromising on tenets you have held nonnegotiable for yourself. No matter how vigilant you are as a coach, the competing demands of the job ensure a certain inevitability when it comes to stepping over the lines we set for ourselves. I have been in this confusing place, saying to myself, "Wait a minute. What am I doing here?" Here are three examples of coaches executing responsibilities and roles that are incongruent with their coaching belief systems.

1. Max is a literacy coach in an elementary school that has adopted a new, expensive reading program. As Max is largely responsible for the organization of the school's collection of leveled texts for guided reading that are housed in the school bookroom, his administrator thought he was a logical candidate for taking inventory of the classroom ancillary materials for the new program at the end of the school year. Max was glad to help and began visiting classrooms with inventory lists and signing teachers' end-of-the-year paperwork. There were no problems with this task—until he reached a teacher who had misplaced some expensive items. Max then realized the awkward position in which he had put himself and the role of power he had inadvertently assumed.

2. Vonda was a first-year literacy coach who was experienced in and knowledgeable about adult learners. She was skilled at facilitating professional learning, and teachers appreciated the ways she scaffolded them. Recognizing her skill, her administrator asked her to facilitate some professional learning during a faculty meeting. Vonda knew that the topic would be difficult to facilitate with the entire faculty at once and would be better as a topic for grade-level meetings. The challenge of the professional learning was compounded by the fact that the administrator told Vonda about it the day before. Vonda wanted to support her administrator and so she agreed. Not surprisingly, the professional learning did not go well, and teachers were frustrated because they were required to participate in training that was not individualized to their grade-level needs. They perceived that Vonda was involved with planning the context of the professional learning, and some were angry at her.

3. Sarah's administrator wanted a standardized lesson plan format for the whole school. Sarah disagreed with this idea; she felt that giving teachers choices and opportunities to individualize lesson plans would increase their planning energy. However, Sarah knew that her administrator was moving forward with or without Sarah's involvement. Sarah also knew that she was more closely connected to the practices in the classroom and would be able to develop a template that was not too cumbersome for teachers, so she agreed to develop a form for her administrator. However, because Sarah developed the form, she understood it better than her administrator, so it soon fell to her to explain the template to the teachers. Understandably, teachers then felt that they should go to Sarah to petition for changes in the form or to see if they were doing it "right." Sarah suddenly felt that she was in an administrative role and was uncomfortable with the evolution of the responsibilities to which she had committed herself.

Coaching Connection: Wet Cement in the Threshold

The examples detailed in the previous section illustrate the ways a coach can accidentally take on a supervisory role. These missteps can be even more dramatic when a literacy coach takes a coaching position that is dramatically incongruent with his or her philosophies of teaching, learning, and coaching. The topic of missteps reminds me of an experience my husband had when he was living in New York City. He once had some business to take care of in a federal building in Manhattan. While he was inside, the city actually poured a new sidewalk extending from the front door; however, they failed to post any "wet cement" signs near the exit. My husband's first steps out of the building were into very wet cement, into which he sank to the middle of his rather long shins.

Given the confusion around the role of literacy coaches and the critical nature of early coaching decisions, new coaches run the risk of taking their very first steps into "wet cement." Consider this section's tools, your "Wet Cement!" signs. The very first task of a new literacy coach should be to clarify his or her role, that is, to make sure the cement has hardened before stepping into new tasks. The effort of looking before you step is worth the time invested.

You do not have to hurry and work with teachers. Get involved with the work of one or two teachers, reflect and learn from this experience, and move forward from there. As a coach, you would be wise to think more than you act, particularly when you are just getting started. There are many places to step into "wet cement" when you are beginning as a coach. Tread lightly.

Resources to Help You Define and Clarify Your Role

Three Great Books About Literacy Coaching

1. *The Literacy Coach's Survival Guide: Essential Questions and Practical Answers* by Cathy A. Toll (2005) is one of my favorite coaching books. This is true partly because it was the first coaching book I ever read, and I am a bit sentimental about it. Mostly, this is true because Cathy hits exactly the right balance between theory and practical application. This book has become a literacy coaching classic.

2. Another favorite literacy coaching book is *Becoming a Literacy Leader: Supporting Learning and Change* by Jennifer Allen (2006). Jennifer has a wonderful voice as a writer and uses it to share relevant, applicable information. It is one of the rare professional books that you can put on your nightstand and read for pleasure and one of three (including this book and *Coaching for Balance)* written by a practicing literacy coach.

3. I strongly recommend Jim Knight's (2007) *Instructional Coaching: A Partnership Approach to Improving Instruction*. I include Jim's book because the "partnership" mentioned in the title is supported throughout the text. Jim Knight's content consistently aligns with a strengths-based philosophy of working with teachers.

Taking Chapter 1 Personally: How Are You Defining and Clarifying *Your* Role?

Questions for Further Reflection

- What do you believe about literacy coaching, and how do these beliefs translate into your actual practice as a coach?

- How do the understandings you have of your job align with the understandings and expectations of your administrator and your district? How do you know?

- How will you be evaluated? Are your efforts as a coach aligned with the evaluation instrument or process in your school district? How are you documenting this alignment?

Possible Action Steps

- Go online and search "literacy coach job description." This will give you a selection of job descriptions that you can review. Use these to inform your development of a new job description or to refine or compare with your current one.

- Obtain a copy of your job description. Take a few minutes to reflect on each of the elements of your evaluation instrument. Identify the areas where you need to invest more time and energy.

CHAPTER 2

Stepping Into the Work of Literacy Coaching

"So be sure when you step. Step with care and great tact and remember that Life's a Great Balancing Act."
Dr. Seuss

Opening Thoughts: Big Shoes

Recently in a professional learning session for coaches, the facilitator asked us, "What are you doing to step into the challenge of this year?" I may be stretching her metaphor beyond her intentions, but I like the idea that we step into a challenge like we step into a pair of shoes. The challenges of literacy coaches are colossal, representing breadth and depth that require us to take risks. Chief among them is the challenge of orienting teachers to your work.

Johnson-Lambert, whose research I presented in the previous chapter, found that the ways literacy coaches share with teachers the nature of literacy coaching made a tremendous difference in the relationships the coaches and teachers developed. She found that coaches are more likely to be successful if they clearly communicate their roles with teachers and that, where communication was limited, teachers and coaches made assumptions of each other, often to the detriment of the coaching program.

The tools in this chapter are designed to help you realize clarity in your interactions with teachers. These tools offer tangible ways to inform teachers of the ways you can help them. They also offer opportunities for you to collect from teachers information that can inform your practice. Whether through presentations at faculty meetings, letters of explanation, newsletters detailing support options, or individual conversations with teachers, literacy coaches are wise to widely distribute information about their work and establish space in teachers' professional learning paradigms. Clarity of communication is critical in the earliest moments of your work but isn't important only for beginning coaches. Seasoned coaches should revisit their role with the faculty at the launch of each new school year, and these tools can support their endeavors as well.

Coaching Connection: Sitting Big

Establishing yourself as part of teachers' frameworks for professional learning requires that coaches make their presence, philosophy, and intention public early. Recently I had an experience that made me think of these critical early days as a coach. I was in a bookstore looking for a book for my son, and I ran across (quite literally) a teacher who was selecting books for her classroom. She was spread out across the aisle, with dozens of books in piles and strewn across the floor. She said, "Excuse me, I'm sitting big." And then she apologized. Of course, as I have "sat big" in a number of bookstores, there was no apology necessary. I appreciated her thoughtfulness, the way she was working from a list of children's names and interests, the way she had sorted books into piles, and the way she was claiming space to engage in her work.

"Sitting big" represents the first and crucial work of literacy coaches who are trying to establish professional relationships with teachers and support the development of learning communities in the school. As a literacy coach, particularly in the early days of your work, I encourage you to "sit big." Take the time to spread out and establish your role in the school in thoughtful ways. Having a literacy coach can dramatically influence the culture of the school, so these early impressions are important. Make room in your schedule and in your physical environment for you to think, and support teachers as they notice, understand, and appreciate you and your role.

Related Research: What Can a Coach Do for You?

While you are sharing with teachers the dimensions of your role, you might want to communicate a little research that supports your presence in a school. One of the most widely referenced pieces of research related to coaching is the meta-analysis of professional learning conducted by Bruce Joyce and Beverly Showers (2002). Table 1, from Joyce and Showers, illustrates the levels of learning attained by professional learning participants in different contexts. For example, just 10% of teachers who only studied the theoretical elements of a new strategy actually demonstrated knowledge, 5% demonstrated skill, and 0% reached full implementation. Even after practicing a new strategy, only 5% of teachers actually implemented the strategy fully. On the other hand, of educators

Table 1
Training Components and Attainment of Outcomes in Terms of Percent of Participants

Components	Outcomes		
	Knowledge (thorough)	Skill (strong)	Transfer (executive implementation)
Study of theory	10	5	0
Demonstrations	30	20	0
Practice	60	60	5
Peer coaching	95	95	95

From Joyce, B.R., & Showers, B. (2002). *Student achievement through staff development.* Alexandria, VA: Association for Supervision and Curriculum Development. Reprinted with permission.

who worked with a coach, 95% reached "executive implementation." I know a number of coaches who share this chart with the faculties in their schools at the beginning of each school year.

Tools for Stepping Into the Work of Literacy Coaching

Orientation to Tool 5: Professional Learning Needs Assessment

I have been a literacy coach for the last five years. This year, my position has changed, and, while I am still coaching in literacy, I am now coaching in math, science, and social studies as well. I recently attended a math workshop and was dismayed to learn that we would be spending the first day of class taking a math test. While I felt vulnerable in this context, I did appreciate the instructional skill our facilitator was demonstrating. All effective teachers find out what their students know before they begin teaching them.

The following tool is designed to help you gather data about what the teachers in your school need in the area of professional learning. I really like the open-endedness of the questions and the qualitative nature of the data it helps you gather.

While the first question hints at a new relationship with a teacher or faculty member, this questionnaire is appropriate even for teachers with whom you have worked for a while and whom you know well. Because, like the other tools in this book, it is rooted in a strengths perspective and because it is open-ended, it serves as a reflective tool for teachers as well as a means of communication between teachers and coach.

PROFESSIONAL LEARNING NEEDS ASSESSMENT

Name _____ Grade/subject _____

Tell me about yourself and your teaching.

What are your areas of strength?

Describe the professional learning that has been most valuable to you in the past.
What made it valuable?

In which instructional area(s) would you like professional learning this year?

Orientation to Tool 6: The Literacy Coaching Opportunities List

Not only did my coaching role expand to include all content areas this year but also my position changed from school level to district level. The organizational structure of the district coaches in my school system is built with a lead coach in each content area who is available to "coach the coaches." Recently I was struggling with planning various professional learning events in my school and I needed another person to help me problem solve, so I called my coach, Barbara Michalove. Seven years ago, as a classroom teacher, I worked with a literacy coach, but I had forgotten how relevant and helpful the support of a skilled coach can be. My coach truly helped me solve my own dilemmas by listening, asking questions, and offering her insight.

This experience of coaching from the other side really gave me perspective into this tool. Working with a coach is truly an opportunity! Having someone to help you accomplish your professional goals and support your growth is a luxury. The Literacy Coaching Opportunities List casts coaching in this positive light. It was created by Alexa Pearson while working in the Centennial School District in Portland, Oregon, USA, and it simply explains what coaches do and who might benefit from working with a coach.

I appreciate Alexa's use of the word *opportunities*. In fact, Alexa's language throughout this list is thoughtful and reflective of her efforts to clearly communicate with teachers that she can support them in ways that will help them meet their goals. In addition to its positive assumption, the Opportunities List is clear and simple.

THE LITERACY COACHING
OPPORTUNITIES LIST

Who Could Work With a Coach?
Teachers who
- Want to implement new literacy strategies in their classroom
- Have questions about something in their classroom
- Want feedback about an issue
- Want to see how something is demonstrated before trying it in the classroom
- Need literacy-related resources for their specific content area
- Have questions about literacy assessment
- Are struggling with some aspect of their class
- Want an extra set of eyes in their classroom

Types of Support Available
Short, focused coaching conferences
- 15–20 minutes
- Focusing on a particular issue
- Brainstorming how you might use a coach

Demonstration lessons
- Watching the literacy coach teach in your classroom
- Watching in a peer's classroom
- Teaching a lesson with the literacy coach (team teaching)

Resource gathering and sharing
- Collecting teaching materials such as graphic organizers or trade books
- Collecting professional reading materials
- Summarizing research or data
- Making contact with other content area teachers
- Developing literacy assessments
- Aligning lessons with reading/writing standards

Classroom visits
- Focusing on an area you select
- Supporting NOT evaluating
- Honoring confidences (unless permission to share positive with others)

Staff development
- Providing professional learning for the whole staff
- Supporting a professional learning community
- Facilitating small-group collaboration and study
- Helping individuals set and meet learning goals

Created by Alexa Pearson.

Practical Literacy Coaching: A Collection of Tools to Support Your Work by Jan Miller Burkins.
© 2009 International Reading Association. May be copied for classroom use.

Orientation to Tool 7: The Literacy Coaching Menu of Services

Once again, the contributors to this book demonstrate thoughtful use of language. This tool is a logical companion to the previous tool, the Literacy Coaching Opportunities List. I think that this menu of services is among the most valuable, elegantly simple forms in this book. I selected it for inclusion in this book because it invites teachers to take action, yet it is supportive enough to make it safe for them to take risks.

When you give this form to teachers, you say in effect, Tell me how I can best support you. Pam Jackson, a middle school literacy coach in the South Lane School District in Cottage Grove, Oregon, developed this menu and her use of the word *services* clearly illustrates that a coach is interested in working beside a teacher and is not serving in an evaluative capacity. Particularly with your initial work with teachers, the subtleties of language can make a tangible difference in the responsiveness of teachers.

While this menu of services is inviting and deferential, it also asks teachers to commit to working with a coach. By distributing this tool to all of the teachers in your school and by asking them all to give some indication of preference (even if that preference is just for more information), you enlist teachers in working with you. Furthermore, the commitment to a time frame at the bottom of the form compels teachers to action and gives you a specific starting place with individual teachers, as well as data to study and consider as you plan for professional learning across your school.

THE LITERACY COACHING MENU OF SERVICES

Dear Teachers:

Below you will find a menu of services or possible ways that I can help you in your literacy efforts this year. Consider which of these services would be most helpful to you, and consider what timeline would work best for you. Please place a check before the "menu items" you are definitely interested in and a question mark before those about which you would like to learn more.

I look forward to working with you this year!

Name _____

_____ Coplanning lessons

_____ Demonstration lessons (in your classroom or visiting one in another teacher's classroom)

_____ New curriculum implementation

_____ Lesson study

_____ Side-by-side coaching/team teaching

_____ Professional text study/ implementation of strategies outlined in text

_____ Viewing instructional videos and planning implementation of new strategies

_____ Videotaping and viewing lesson(s)

_____ Classroom visit to help brainstorm

_____ Meet with grade levels or teams to address solutions for a specific question, share information, etc.

_____ Assist in the creation of a professional development plan in your classroom based on student data

_____ Brainstorm ways to combine technology and literacy

_____ Brainstorm ways to conference with each student during the writing process

_____ Organize/arrange classroom seating/ working areas to make it more conducive to meet your instructional goals

_____ Provide support and assistance with reading instruction, assessment, and data analysis

_____ Provide information about conferences that address questions you have about instructional practices in literacy

_____ Other

_____

_____

_____

_____ Other

_____

_____

_____

I would like support
_____ immediately _____ within the next 2 months _____ let's meet to plan a time

The best time for me to meet with a coach is (please write the time in the blank)
_____ before school _____ after school _____ planning time _____ other

---

Created by Pam Jackson.

Practical Literacy Coaching: A Collection of Tools to Support Your Work by Jan Miller Burkins.

Orientation to Tool 8: Literacy Coaching Newsletter

Literacy coaches inevitably find themselves collecting details to communicate with teachers. For me, these accumulate on lists and sticky notes that paper my workspace. Most of the entries on these notes will eventually make it into e-mails directed to individuals, but sometimes I am concerned that these communications are inefficient or redundant.

As an alternative, Instructional Coach Brian Madej lets a weekly, electronic newsletter do the heavy lifting of his miscellaneous communication with teachers. A sample newsletter, "Reading Matters," is featured in Tool 8. Brian finds that teachers appreciate that he does not bombard them with e-mail and that they rely on the predictability with which the newsletter arrives in their inboxes each Friday. Because Brian fills the newsletter with information that is relevant for teachers, they are inclined to read it. Each week, he follows a predictable format so that teachers know where to look to find the information most relevant for them.

In addition to sending out the newsletter electronically, Brian posts each week's newsletter in a folder on a shared drive. This means that teachers have easy access to "back issues" and can refer to them as needed.

I have experimented with developing a newsletter as Brian does. I find that if I begin it early in the week and keep it open as I complete other computer work, then it is pretty much finished by the end of the week when I am ready to send it out. Furthermore, typing information for teachers onto a newsletter as concerns and questions arise saves me time, because I don't make notes and then later transfer them to e-mail.

LITERACY COACHING NEWSLETTER

Reading Matters

A Weekly Update from Your Literacy Coach

Questions that have surfaced this week:

Friday, October 31st, 2008

- **Where are the books for the fluency assessments?** They are located in the bookroom on the shelf directly inside the door. They are sorted by level. Timers are there for check-out as well.

- **What resources do we have to support our informational writing?** We have a number of excellent resources that include mini-lessons, and even entire units, for supporting informational writing. I have pulled them all together and put them on the resource shelf in the library.

- **How often do we need to do running records?** We have committed to administering a running record to one child each day. This means that, roughly we will have one running record for each child each month.

Coach's General Schedule for Next Week

Monday—Demonstration Lessons, a.m.; Planning-p.m.

Tuesday—Guided Reading Classroom Visits

Wednesday— First-grade Guided Reading Demos a.m.; teacher conferences, p.m.; "Language as Action" study group, afternoon

Thursday—Grade-level Team Meetings, All Day

Friday—Coach's Meeting @ BOE

Grade-Level Updates

All Grades: Forty-five Day Action Plans are due the central office on November 17th. If you would like help analyzing your data or developing instructional strategies, please let me know.

Benchmarking copies have been replenished and are filed by level on the bookshelf in my office. Help yourself to copies!

Kindergarten: Copies of the formative assessments for literacy are at the print-shop. They should be back sometime next week.

First-grade: There have been updates to the **district curriculum maps.** If you need help accessing these online, let me know.

Third-grade: You should go ahead and begin collecting writing samples for the **state writing assessment** during your information writing unit. Please, let me know how I can support you.

Upcoming Professional Learning Events!

Monday, November 3rd: PLANNING DAY! No meetings scheduled, but if you want support with planning, please let me know!

Wednesday, November 5th: The "Language as Action" study group is meeting from 2:45-3:45. Please, read Chapter 2 of *Choice Words* by Peter Johnston.

Thursday, November 6th: Professional Learning Day for 1st Grade! Please, bring your computers, your running record notebooks, and a student writing sample.

Have You Checked This Out?

The Department of Education website has an amazing amount of great info. I have just begun clicking around and found lesson plans, resources, teaching videos in all content areas, and all sorts of helpful stuff. Please take some time (yeah, right!) and poke around! Check out these exceptionally cool features: www.georgiastandards.org

Elluminate Live: An instructional chat room to address any and all teaching issues.

Teacher Tools Menu: (at the left on the main page) great websites to support the classroom

State Units: These have been developed to support the GPS.

CRCT Content Descriptors: http://public.doe.k12.ga.us/ci_testing.aspx?PageReq=CITestingCRCTDesc

Created by Brian Madej and Jan Miller Burkins.

A Coaching Story: Quality Over Quantity

Once upon a time there was a teacher, we'll call her Laura, who became a literacy coach and was—as most coaches are, particularly at the onset of a position—eager to be invited to join in the work of teachers. She wanted early to establish trust and build relationships. So Laura spread herself through the building in service to teachers.

One would think that any action in service of teachers would build relationships, and it did to some extent. However, although rolling up your sleeves and helping a teacher sort through his or her classroom library is deep and meaningful work of service, it is possible to commit yourself to such a multitudinous collection of random tasks that you find yourself working in a role that is primarily clerical and does little to promote the professional growth of teachers. This was the position in which Laura found herself.

Furthermore, such responsibilities are easier to step into than they are to climb out of. Laura found that as she tried to shed the tasks she had taken on, resentment built among teachers. It is significant as well that while Laura was engaging in efforts that were time-consuming and physically demanding, she was unable to engage in the more consequential efforts that might have affected classroom instruction and student learning more significantly. So, not only was she investing personal resources in efforts with little payoff, she was losing ground with teachers in other capacity-building ways.

In the end, Laura decided that coaching was not for her. Although her efforts to launch her work in her school were sincere, I wonder now how her literacy coaching experience might have been different if she had worked to make sure that her support of teachers was focused around promoting professional growth. This is not to say that coaches should not help teachers with the labor-intensive work of organizing classrooms and instruction; sometimes this is the most meaningful work a coach can do to establish relationships with teachers. It simply means that teachers have to think of the "big picture" of their coaching efforts and be careful to consider the long-term effects of their time distributions.

Coaching Connection: One Piece at a Time

Part of what led Laura to rush her early work with teachers was pressure to reach an end result quickly. Certainly, it is easy to focus on the outcome of an effort rather than the process of getting there. My son taught me a lesson about this recently. My 5-year-old, Natie, is fascinated by Legos and can entertain himself with them for hours. He has just discovered the gratification that comes from working through a kit that guides him step by step through a process where he ends up with an airplane, a boat, or a motorcycle.

Recently, he was working on a particularly complicated Lego project, one he had borrowed from his 12-year-old brother. He came down to show me his progress and I admired the design, still yet unrecognizable as the helicopter it would become. I asked, "What step are you on?" He said, "Seven." Then, revealing my own tendencies to focus on the end rather than the process, I asked, "How many steps are there in all?" He paused and then responded, "I don't know." I was incredulous, "You mean you haven't looked to see how many steps there are to make the whole helicopter?" He looked at me and said matter-of-factly, "No. It really doesn't matter, does it?"

Sometimes the work of literacy coaching can be truly overwhelming. Particularly when we are just getting started, there is so much that we want to influence in classrooms that it is easy to focus on the vastness of the work. At times, all we can see is how far we have to go. However, if we can focus our work on processes, thinking of each step as an end in itself, we can find more satisfaction in our work. I am aware that this can be a tremendous challenge, particularly in the face of standardized tests that are set up as the final step in our work. However, even this all-important "final" product can stand to be viewed through a lens that allows us to enjoy the steps rather than count them down.

Resources for Stepping Into Your Work as Literacy Coach

Three Excellent Websites for Literacy Coaches

1. The website that I access the most is Choice Literacy (www .choiceliteracy.com). It offers a wealth of resources about coaching and literacy. Jennifer Allen frequently writes for the site, and I find that her philosophy aligns with mine. Brenda Power, the developer of Choice Literacy, writes a free weekly newsletter, which is inspiring and filled with links to other resources. There is a small membership fee, but Choice Literacy also offers free resources that are described in the weekly newsletter.

2. The site I access almost as much as Choice Literacy is the National School Reform Faculty's website (www.nsrfharmony.org). Their mission is to further the work of Facilitative Leadership and Critical Friends in schools. Critical Friends is a specific, week-long professional learning event in which educators can learn ways to facilitate and participate in inquiry-based professional learning. However, you don't have to formally participate in Critical Friends to utilize the array of resources on their

website. Among other unique content, the site includes an alphabetical list of protocols that you can use to facilitate professional learning. I highly recommend using these in your work with teachers. For more information about Critical Friends Groups, see *Tools for Leaders* by Marjorie Larner (2007), which also presents a collection of Critical Friends protocols.

3. The Literacy Coaching Clearinghouse (www.literacycoachingonline .org) is a joint effort of the National Council of Teachers of English and IRA. Its mission is "to enhance the important work of literacy coaches, reading coaches, reading specialists, and instructional coaches as they strive to increase the quality of teacher instruction and student achievement" (¶ 1). It includes blogs, a list of events of value to coaches, a collection of research briefs, and an exhaustive list of resources for coaches, including every book ever written about literacy coaching.

Taking Chapter 2 Personally: How Are You Stepping Into *Your* Work as Literacy Coach?

Questions for Reflection

- How do the understandings you have of your job align with the literacy coaching understandings and expectations of the teachers with whom you work? How do you know?

- What are you doing to inform teachers of the dimensions of your role as literacy coach? How do you know they understand?

- What are your goals for the beginning of the school year? How did you decide on these goals?

Possible Action Steps

- Meet with your administrator to discuss the ways you want to present your role to the faculty in your school. Share with your principal any handouts you are going to use. Discuss how he or she can support your communication with the faculty. Schedule time to present in an upcoming faculty meeting.

- Use the Literacy Coaching Menu of Services to gather data from the faculty. Take the data and compile it and share it with the faculty. Use the data to develop an action plan for yourself. Share the action plan with your administrator.

CHAPTER 3

Stretching Yourself

"Our lives improve only when we take chances—and the first and most difficult risk we can take is to be honest with ourselves."
Walter Anderson

Opening Thoughts: Risky Business

Literacy coaching is difficult and dangerous work. There is daily risk associated with changing ourselves and asking others to join us. However, it is not unusual for a literacy coach to fall into a predictable, comfortable rhythm of facilitation and classroom visitation. Patterns of classroom support emerge and we, like teachers, can find ourselves in learning ruts.

So much of our effort is focused on the willingness of others to learn and change, and our time for our own reflection is often scant. So, while we can be quick to register some teachers' hesitancy to change, many of us experience a natural tentativeness as well when a piece of professional literature or a colleague asks us to embrace some new coaching practice or questions our beliefs about literacy coaching. Our reactions reflect those of teachers, as we slip into the natural good–bad binary and ask, "What do you mean I have been doing this coaching thing the *wrong* way?" However, we know that professionalism demands that we see beyond black–white rationalism and embrace the muddiness of varying contexts and perspectives.

This chapter encourages you to give yourself a bit of attention and invest the personal energy necessary to push yourself to the edge of your learning. Recognize your discomfort zones and step into them. If you find this challenging—and you naturally will—invite someone you trust to push you into these frightening spaces. If the work you are initiating is not at least a little unsettling and if it doesn't involve at least some risk, then you are probably limiting yourself. So set up scaffolding structures beneath yourself, employ the support of your colleagues, and venture out in ways that are risky for you. Court failure because such risks hold promise of life-changing breakthroughs.

Coaching Connection: Coaches Worth Their Salt

Attending to your professional learning as I am suggesting is expensive in a number of ways. Most literally, if you take your annual salary and break it down to an hourly rate, you are probably among the better paid educators in your school. Most literacy coaches have extra degrees and extra years of experience, which costs districts extra funding. Based on this, I sometimes like to think about how I am spending my time and scrutinize my schedule through a district's accounting lens by asking: Is the district getting its money's worth when I do this work?

Granted, for most of us, we put in so many extra hours that if you calculated an actual hourly wage we are making about $1.25 an hour. Nevertheless, it is worth considering our time expenditures as they relate to the value they offer to the school and district. In light of this cost analysis, how do we justify spending time on our own professional learning and reflection?

Recently, I was watching *CBS Sunday Morning* (Morrison, 2008) with Charles Osgood, a Sunday ritual for me, and it presented a piece on the history of salt. Apparently, salt comes in an array of colors, flavors, and forms. The interviewer, Martha Teichner, asked the salt expert, David Bitterman, what would you say to the person who asks, "Why should I spend much, much more money to buy fancy salt rather than going to the store and buying a little cardboard carton?"" He replied, "Because every single thing you eat will taste better." The interviewer was taken aback, and so was I; I can't argue with such all-encompassing logic. Pass the pink salt, please.

As a literacy coach, the professional learning and reflection in which you participate is the salt you sprinkle on your work; it will make everything you do better. Yes, in terms of time, reflection is expensive, but the district's return on their money is considerable. If you are not presently strategic about your own professional learning, let this chapter and these tools spur you to action.

Related Research: Reflecting With Others

Usually, reflection is considered a solitary activity. Efforts to consider our work are usually measured against paradigms we already have in place. While individual reflection is, in my opinion, worthwhile, it has some inherent flaws. How deeply can we reflect without a new paradigm against which we can measure ourselves?

P. Taylor Webb (2001) maintains that "reflection as a process of thinking alone does not account for the beliefs and biases that guide the thinking in the first place" (p. 246). Thus, the most valuable reflection is in conjunction with an "other" (a text, a coach, a mentor, etc.) who might question our beliefs and thinking. Co-reflection serves as a means to interrogate our beliefs about teaching and learning (Burkins & Ritchie, 2007). Webb continues, "It is important to stress how reflection is implicated with the same attitudes it is attempting to uncover" (p. 246).

Thus, reflection that is dialogic in nature serves to offset the biases that influence our self-reflection. Such reflection exchanges create what Laura Robb (2000) refers to as "knowledge-building partnerships" (p. 52) and invites literacy coaches to engage in more demanding reflection toward the end of greater professional growth. This type of intense reflection requires dialogue between literacy coaches and, by capitalizing on the social nature of learning (Vygotsky, 1934/1962), facilitates the type of stretching and growth that are the topic of this chapter, progress that might be impeded by the level of comfort and familiarity inherent in examining one's practice against the paradigms that already support it.

I have found Webb's premise to be true for my practice. Historically, I have experienced the most profound growth when I have had a reflective partner who is willing to say, "Oh, yeah, Jan? How do you know?" and "What about these competing ideas?" For this reason, the tools in this section open with a structure for collaborating and reflecting with a trusted coaching colleague to explore the ways that social–professional interactions can support your growth.

Tools for Stretching Yourself

Orientation to Tool 9: The Coach-to-Coach Cycle

A literacy coach's attention to his or her professional learning may be the variable that most contributes to his or her longevity as a coach. Literacy coaching is a challenging profession and to make it even more difficult, there are few well-designed professional learning opportunities for literacy coaches. It is easy for coaches to neglect themselves and burn out.

To address these problems, I recommend that a literacy coach set aside time weekly to attend to his or her own reflection and professional growth. This time can be spent reading, exploring professional learning topics with other coaches, and engaging in exercises such as those that follow here.

The Coach-to-Coach Cycle (Burkins & Ritchie, 2007) is simply a structure by which two literacy coaches can coach each other. Scott

Ritchie and I developed this structure and found it a tremendously valuable way to support and push each other. In this protocol, one coach serves as the guest coach who is going to support the home coach in a classroom visit and the series of conferences that encompass it. While the home coach talks with the teacher, the guest coach scripts the dialogue in the same way he or she would script the language of a classroom observation (for more on scripting, see "A Coaching Story: Learning to Script Lessons" in Chapter 5).

For each level of conferring (pre- and postconferences), the guest coach and the home coach engage in dialogue, plan before each step, and reflect. In each stage, the collaborating coaches use their scripts to support their conversations. This tool illustrates each step in the Coach-to-Coach Cycle. See Burkins and Ritchie, 2007, for a more comprehensive description of the process.

THE COACH-TO-COACH CYCLE

Meeting	Guest coach	Home coach	Classroom teacher	Purpose
1. Prior to preobservation conference	Engages in dialogue and gathers information, documents coaching goals of the home coach	Engages in dialogue and articulates goals, both as a coach and specifically for the preobservation conference	Not present	To organize thoughts and plan upcoming coach–teacher preobservation conference
2. Preobservation conference	Observes and scripts the home coach's interaction with the teacher	Engages in dialogue with teacher, gathers information about teacher's goals for the lesson and focus for the observation	Engages in dialogue with coach, articulates goals for the lesson and focus for the observation	To establish purposes for classroom visit
3. After preobservation conference/ before observation	Engages in dialogue; shares notes from preconference, particularly those related to literacy coach's goals; may share insights on teacher's goals	Engages in dialogue with guest coach, reflects on preobservation conference as it relates to professional goals, clarifies priorities for observation	Not present	To reflect on preobservation conference as it relates to observation
4. Classroom visit	Observes instruction, takes notes, and scripts teacher–student interactions	Observes instruction, takes notes, and scripts teacher–student interactions	Teaches lesson	To gather anecdotal notes for reflection

(continued)

THE COACH-TO-COACH CYCLE
(continued)

Meeting	Guest coach	Home coach	Classroom teacher	Purpose
5. Analysis and interpretation	Analyzes and engages in dialogue about observational data (notes and transcript), helps home coach set goals for postobservation conference with teacher	Analyzes and engages in dialogue about observational data (notes and transcript), sets goals for postobservation conference with teacher	Not present	To reflect on notes from classroom visit as they relate to the goals of the teacher and the home coach
6. Postobservation conference	Observes home coach–teacher interactions, scripts home coach's words	Engages in dialogue with teacher, reflects on observation as relates to teacher's professional learning goals	Participates in postobservation conference, reflects on observation as relates to goals	To document home coach's interactions with teachers related to specific goals
7. After postobservation conference	Reflects on post-observation conference, reviews notes related to the home coach's professional goals	Reflects on post-observation conference in relation to goals of coach and teacher	Not present	To reflect on previous action in order to inform next Coach-to-Coach Cycle, to set new goals for work with the teacher and for the home coach in general
8. After entire cycle	Debriefs process and plans next cycle	Debriefs process and plans next cycle	Not present	To reflect on process and plan to start next cycle

Burkins, J.M., & Ritchie, S. (2007). Coaches coaching coaches. *Journal of Language and Literacy Education*, 3(1), p. 39. Reprinted with permission.

Orientation to Tool 10:
Language-Scrutinizing Exercise

The most critical element in literacy coaching is relationships, and these are nurtured or squashed through the words we choose in our day-to-day interactions with teachers. Of particular importance is the way we communicate about teacher growth and change. The nature of your word choices is potentially powerful when it comes to building or hindering progress in your school. Our words are much like bridges that can link us to teachers and build connections across the school. The following exercise is included as a self-study or a costudy with a fellow literacy coach. I offer it as a way for you to support your own professional growth.

Exercises such as this work much the way that physical exercise works to influence our lives beyond the gym or beyond an exercise class. For example, practicing yoga a couple of times a week can have an impact on my posture or the way I carry myself throughout the rest of the week. In this language-scrutinizing exercise, you have the opportunity to engage in some deep, reflective work with the possibility of payoff that translates into changes in your habituated practices. Most important, this exercise holds the potential to set in motion a constant reflective stance that will help you scrutinize the language you use with teachers.

Much of what we say in our interactions with teachers comes from a level of automaticity. That is, our language is embedded in habituated word choices and patterns of response. Breaking or improving these habits requires bringing less effective language patterns to a conscious level. This work is challenging, but the efforts offer tremendous opportunities both for you and for the teachers in your school.

LANGUAGE-SCRUTINIZING EXERCISE

Words are powerful, and the ways we use them have an impact on our lives in and out of school. The purpose of this exercise is to think reflectively about the language of coaching. This activity is not designed to define the "right" or "wrong" way to facilitate a group or coach a teacher. The intent, instead, is to support coaches as they think critically about their word choices so that their understandings of their own speech can inform their conversations with teachers.

For this exercise, the coach must record and transcribe a conversation with a teacher. Postobservation conferences lend themselves to language scrutiny and usually provide much fodder for examination. An alternative to recording and transcribing is asking another literacy coach to script the conversation. The coaches can analyze the script together, if they are comfortable with this, and then switch roles. Another option is practicing this analysis with a coaching transcript from a published resource such as those in Marilyn Duncan's (2006) book, *Literacy Coaching: Developing Effective Teachers Through Instructional Dialogue*.

Part I: Raising the Level of the Interaction/Coaching Toward Independence
Read your script for examples of each of the following. Work with your partner to explore how you might have used language differently.

   A. "Good job."—Using phrases like "That's right" or "Good job" places the coach in a position of power. "Good" is a value judgment, and it implies that the coach knows the "right" way to teach. Read your script for places where you have made value judgments.

   Reflection:

   B. Questions or directions that narrow or end the conversation—This might be questions that lead the participants or questions that have a "right" answer. Read your script for places where you have narrowed the conversation.

   Reflection:

(continued)

C. Entry points—Where did the coach prompt the teacher? How smooth were these transitions? Were there missed opportunities where the teacher gave the coach a chance to support, but the coach missed it? Was the coach too pushy? Read your script for places to open conversation.

Reflection:

D. The heart of the exchange or the shift in thinking—Look for places where there seemed to be an "aha!" Where is the big idea of the event? What was the primary understanding of the group? What role did the facilitator play in arriving at these understandings? Read your script for places of discovery.

Reflection:

Part II: Sorting and Naming the Language
Examine the language of your facilitation and look for patterns. Look beyond the language and try to identify the purpose of each statement. Group statements based on commonalities in purpose and label the categories. (Sometimes using different-colored highlighters can help with this.)

What were your categories? In which category did the majority of your language fit? What patterns did you notice?

Reflection:

Orientation to Tool 11: Questions and Stems for Coaching Conversations

In my opinion, the key to effective conferences with teachers is striking that balance between asking and telling. There are many views on coaching conferences. Some suggest that coaches should never make suggestions to teachers but that teachers should arrive at their own conclusions about their instruction and what they can do to improve. This philosophy is often framed as inquiry. I appreciate this philosophy; however, it can be hard to execute. Oftentimes the coach has some ideas that will help the teacher, but rather than just sharing the suggestions, the coach engages the teacher in an "inquiry" process that is basically the teacher trying to guess what the coach is thinking. Such conferences translate into a series of hints from the coach and guesses from the teacher.

Mike Schmoker (2006) bemoans the fact that teachers get so little straightforward feedback on their instruction. He writes, "We have to take responsibility for the message this lack of feedback sends to teachers: that teaching, the soul of their chosen profession, doesn't much matter" (p. 27). Certainly, work as important as teaching deserves genuine feedback support.

At the other extreme, there are coaches and supporting literature that actually step into an evaluative stance and tell teachers exactly what to do in their classrooms. Such extreme exchanges blur the line between coaching and administration and communicate a lack of respect for the expertise of the teacher. In addition, they can compromise the coach–teacher relationship.

In an effort to find a middle ground between these two extremes, my strategy has been to try to strike a balance between supporting teachers as they reflect on their instruction and offering them some insight that comes from being an additional set of eyes. This is a struggle, and I don't always find this balance; it is easier to achieve in theory than in reality. However, the key for me has been having some sound questions ready.

Most every book on literacy coaching has a section on asking questions. Many even have lists similar to this one (cf. Crane, 2002, pp. 128 and 103; Dozier, 2006, p. 40; Lyons & Pinnell, 2001, p. 164). I have divided this list into sections and placed in italics the questions I ask most.

QUESTIONS AND STEMS
FOR COACHING CONVERSATIONS

Questions that invite elaboration
- Why do you say that?
- What do you mean?
- *Tell me more.*
- Describe the thought process behind your decision.
- What else?
- How do you know?
- *I am hearing you say that.... What did I miss?*
- What will you do next?
- Explain that, please.

Questions for preobservation conferences
- What is your primary goal for your lesson today, and how will you know if you have met it?
- On what would you like me to focus my attention while I am watching the lesson?
- What are your students' strengths in this area? Challenges?
- When you imagine yourself as the teacher you want to be, what gets in your way? (Toll, 2005)

Questions for postobservation conferences
- What did you learn from your lesson today?
- What does the students' work tell you about the lesson?
- Were there any tricky parts to your lesson? What were they, and how were they tricky?
- *What was your favorite part of the lesson, and why?*
- *What worked for you and your students in the lesson today?*
- What would you do differently if you taught this lesson again?

Stems for giving positive feedback (something beyond "The lesson was good.")
- Here are some research-based strategies I saw you use today.
- *Here is something I learned from you today.*
- *I saw you.... This is a sound practice because....*
- *I enjoyed being in your classroom today because....*

Stems for making suggestions
- *You might try....*
- Here is something you could consider.
- *Here is something I noticed that might be getting in your way.* (Hindley, 1998)
- Another approach to this might be....

Questions that invite action
- What are your next steps?
- *What do you need from me?*

Orientation to Tool 12: Postobservation Conference Preparation Exercise: A Strengths Perspective

I have always put considerable time into preparing for postobservation conversations. Such conferences have opposing challenges at work within them. How do I know when to tell and when to support teacher inquiry? How do I support inquiry without appearing manipulative? How do I support risk-taking and growth without violating trust? Most important, how do I focus on strengths and propel classrooms toward improvement? The Postobservation Conference Preparation Exercise addresses this last question in particular.

The following reflective exercise is designed to support coaches as they plan for conferences. I have found that the practice of thinking through, even writing out, what I might say to a teacher has helped me develop some automaticity around language that helps me support teachers in ways that influence classroom practice.

In the same way that our earliest lesson plans in undergraduate school were extensive and detailed, the preparation we put into learning to facilitate effective postobservation conferences results in a level of reflection about our work that is later realized on an automatic level.

I have included a completed sample of this form to help you consider the ways it might support you. It is based on an amalgam of lessons I have observed in classrooms and touches on the common challenge of helping teachers support children as they think deeply about what they are reading. This lesson represents something I might see in a K–2 classroom and illustrates one way I might talk with the teacher.

The value of this tool is that it forces a pattern of visitation and reflection that is built around a strengths perspective. Such a focus, which is by definition rooted in an assumption of goodwill, helps develop a community of learning in a school that can affect classroom practice and student learning in tremendous ways.

POSTOBSERVATION CONFERENCE PREPARATION EXERCISE: A STRENGTHS PERSPECTIVE

After visiting a classroom and scripting a lesson, make a copy of the script and use it as a tool to scaffold your reflection.

Step 1: Strengths
What does the teacher do well? Identify and write about the places where the teacher demonstrates skill? Include evidence from the script.

1.

2.

3.

Step 2: Areas of Growth
List three areas of growth for the teacher. Explain.

1.

2.

3.

Step 3: Approximations
Are there any teacher behaviors that are approximations of one of the areas the teacher needs to strengthen (from list above)? Does the teacher seem to already be stretching in one of the areas that needs some attention? List evidence from the script. Area of Focus (selected from list in previous section):

Evidence of approximations:

Step 4: Planning and Reflection
What can you say to the teacher to connect the dots between his or her approximations and the area of growth on which you would like to focus?

(continued)

POSTOBSERVATION CONFERENCE PREPARATION EXERCISE: A STRENGTHS PERSPECTIVE *(continued)*

Step 5: Practicing the Language of Coaching

What will you say to the teacher? In preparation for your conference, write out what you might say to the teacher as you address the area of growth. Be sure to refer to evidence from the script.

How might you initiate the conversation?

What might you say about the strengths you saw in the teacher's lesson?

How might you support the teacher's growth?

How might you wrap up the conference?

Note: This is not a "script" for your postobservation conference but rather a place to practice and be deliberate in thinking about the language of your coaching. Obviously, the postobservation conference should be a conversation, and this exercise is limited to only one side of the exchange.

SAMPLE POSTOBSERVATION CONFERENCE PREPARATION EXERCISE: A STRENGTHS PERSPECTIVE

After visiting a classroom and scripting a lesson, make a copy of the script and use it as a tool to scaffold your reflection.

Step 1: Strengths
What does the teacher do well? Identify and write about the places where the teacher demonstrates skill? Include evidence from the script.

1. *Encourages students to reflect on their reading behaviors*
"You figured that out. I was listening to you. What did you do to figure that out?"
"I heard you make a mistake and then go back and fix it. How did you know that there was a problem?"

2. *Manages the big picture of guided reading (i.e., materials, groups, centers, etc.). Students know procedures and routines.*
Transition to guided reading table took less than five minutes for each rotation. Students knew what to do when they got to the table. They began rereading their book from the previous day as soon as they sat down. There were no management issues with their bags, where to sit, etc. Students working at centers did not interrupt the guided reading lessons.

3. *Keeps anecdotal records of student reading behaviors*
Teacher uses a checklist to record reading behaviors specific to the particular guided reading level. This also indicates that she understands the varying demands of different reading levels.

Step 2: Areas of Growth
List three areas of growth for the teacher. Explain.

1. *Focusing on reading as meaning making; developing comprehension skills in the students*
Students are not efficiently utilizing the pictures to support their reading. They focus on the print with only cursory consideration of the pictures. Consequently, they are missing the deeper story, which is carried by the pictures. The comprehension questions the teacher is asking do not require the students to think deeply about the story.

2. *The introduction to the text needs to be better developed.*
There is little introduction to the text. The teacher simply asks the children to take a "picture walk" through the book and then begin reading. If she sees that several children have a problem with a word, she interrupts them all and goes over the word. She is not activating relevant vocabulary prior to the reading of the text or setting any kind of purpose for reading.

3. *Pacing of lesson*
Each lesson was approximately 40 minutes, which meant that the teacher was unable to get to the struggling group.

(continued)

SAMPLE POSTOBSERVATION CONFERENCE PREPARATION EXERCISE: A STRENGTHS PERSPECTIVE *(continued)*

Step 3: Approximations

Are there any teacher behaviors that are approximations of one of the areas the teacher needs to strengthen (from list above)? Does the teacher seem to already be stretching in one of the areas that needs some attention? List evidence from the script.

Area of Focus (selected from list in previous section): *Reading as meaning making*
Evidence of approximations:
"Be sure to go all the way through the book and look at the pictures first and then go back and start reading the words."
"Evan, you are looking at the pictures very carefully."
Teacher reviews with the students basic elements of narrative stories. She asks them to name the setting, the characters, and the plot.

Step 4: Planning and Reflection

What might you say to the teacher to connect the dots between his or her approximations and the area of growth on which you would like to focus?
The teacher indicates that reading for meaning is a priority for her; however, she does not seem to know how to support that completely. Her prompting leans toward visual cues and, while she makes some references to the "plot" of the story and encourages students to consider the pictures, she does not engage them in this work in a deep way. I don't think she sees the parallel stories embedded in the pictures of these simpler texts. I think that I can point them out to her as a way to support her interest in teaching the students to read thoughtfully. While my conference may focus on meaning making in general, I think I can connect it to the introduction.

Step 5: Practicing the Language of Coaching

What will you say to the teacher? In preparation for your conference, write out what you might say to the teacher as you address the area of growth. Be sure to refer to evidence from the script.

How might you initiate the conversation?
Take a minute and reflect on your lesson. What worked for you and your students? What would you do differently?

What will you say about the strengths you saw in the teacher's lesson?
Here are some things I saw that really seem to be working for you. First, you really have established the routines and procedures surrounding guided reading. This is truly the first challenge to guided reading, figuring out how to engage the children who are not with you and establishing systems for transitioning smoothly from one group to another. Specifically, everyone understood what to do at each of the centers, and the few who had questions did not interrupt your time in guided reading but rather asked a friend for help. This is not an easy behavior to establish with kindergarten children.

(continued)

SAMPLE POSTOBSERVATION CONFERENCE PREPARATION EXERCISE: A STRENGTHS PERSPECTIVE *(continued)*

Another thing that really stuck out to me was your depth of understanding of the reading process in general and of your children's reading processes in particular. The way you encouraged your children to reflect on their strategy work gave you insight into how they were problem solving. For example, here you said, "You figured that out. I was listening to you. What did you do to figure it out?" and then you also talked to Claire; you said, "I heard you make a mistake and then go back and fix it. How did you know that there was a problem?" Then, you took it a step further and documented the behaviors you saw and heard.

How might you support the teacher's growth?

I notice, too, that you are really interested in supporting your students' comprehension and negotiation of the meaning system. Your work with them is not just about decoding the words but about their understanding what they are reading. I saw this a number of times. For example, you encouraged them to look at the pictures before they read. This activates their prior knowledge and focuses them on making sense of the story. You also focused your teaching point around the narrative elements of the story.

To build on this, you could take what you are already doing with the picture work a step further by encouraging them to find the "secret" of the book. If you convey to them that the pictures carry meaning that is not obvious in the words, then it becomes their job to thoughtfully approach the pictures. They become detectives.

Let's look at one of the stories from this morning's lesson. What would be the "secret" of this book?

So while the students comprehended that this story was about a little boy who was scared and that his mother came in to comfort him, they did not notice that the things that scared him were imagined creatures formed from his clothes scattered around the room. You can support them in taking their comprehension to the next level by getting them to really search for the story in the pictures.

How might you wrap up the conference?

I am happy to plan with you, if you would like. Then we could look through guided reading books in the bookroom and think about which ones lend themselves to the kind of thoughtful reading we have been talking about.

Note: This is not a "script" for your postobservation conference but rather a place to practice and be deliberate in thinking about the language of your coaching. Obviously, the postobservation conference should be a conversation, and this exercise is limited to only one side of the exchange.

Orientation to Tool 13:
Coach's Postevent Reflection Guide

After every coaching event, whether it is a conference, a study group, or a whole-faculty professional learning session, most literacy coaches engage in some level of reflection. Considering what worked and what we would change about a particular coaching experience is a natural behavior for most of us. However, natural behaviors can betray patterns that may neglect some dimension of our learning. If I always ask myself the same questions after I work with teachers, what might this automaticity cause me to overlook in my work?

I developed this reflection guide in collaboration with Brian Madej and Kerstin Long, two practicing instructional coaches in my school district. I encourage you to use these questions to broaden your reflection after an experience with teachers. Let some of these new reflective prompts become automatic for you.

What I like most about this tool is its flexibility. Its universal applicability to a variety of literacy coaching interactions makes it more relevant, and its sustained use invites us to expand our habits of mind.

COACH'S POSTEVENT REFLECTION GUIDE

13

1. On a scale of 1–10, with 10 being "The _____ was perfect; I am the best literacy coach in the history of education" and 1 being "That was the most horrible _____ I could even imagine; I'm going into accounting," how would you rate this event? _____ Why?

2. How do you think this _____ affected your relationship with the teacher(s)?

3. How did the _____ vary from your preparation and anticipation of it? To what do you attribute this variation?

4. How did you build on the teacher's (teachers') strengths?

5. How did you manage the balance between supporting inquiry and explicitly telling?

6. What did the teacher(s) commit to doing next? What will you do next to promote and support follow-up action related to this work?

7. What do you think the teacher(s) learned from this experience? What is your evidence?

8. What did you learn from this experience?

Created by Jan Miller Burkins, Brian Madej, and Kerstin Long.

Orientation to Tool 14: Self-Assessment for Elementary Literacy Coaches

With the advent of standards-based instruction, the ways we go about our work are changing. Many school districts require that teachers "post" the standards they are teaching. Part of supporting teachers in these contexts involves helping them self-evaluate the ways their instruction is supporting students as they demonstrate their understanding of particular standards.

Similarly, IRA in collaboration with four content area national councils (and funding from the Carnegie Corporation) has developed standards for middle and high school literacy coaches. You can order these standards from either organization or you can download a copy for free at www .reading.org/downloads/resources/597coaching_standards.pdf. Although they are labeled for middle and high school, these standards are directly applicable to the work of elementary literacy coaches, too.

To help us assess the ways we are meeting our professional standards, the Literacy Coaching Clearinghouse has developed a series of self-assessments for literacy, reading, and instructional coaches. Included here you will find the Self-Assessment for Elementary Literacy Coaches. This is an extensive document that will give you the opportunity to evaluate yourself along nine criteria.

The comprehensive nature of the self-assessment gives you options in how you utilize it. You might complete the entire self-assessment at the beginning of a school year to plan for your professional learning throughout the year. You may modify it by taking one section per month during a school year to examine closely. The rubric for completing the assessment is necessarily detailed. I appreciate this but find I get a little lost in the language when I complete the assessment. You can simplify the process by considering the two extremes, "not sufficiently knowledgeable" and "experienced...and...confident that I can apply similar skills in additional content areas." Hold these two descriptions in your head and plot yourself along a mental continuum between them.

If you are a middle or high school literacy coach, don't feel left out; there is a self-assessment tailored to your special job demands. You can access a self-evaluative tool for middle and high school literacy coaches at www.literacycoachingonline.org/library/resources/self-assessmentformshs literacycoaches.html.

SELF-ASSESSMENT FOR ELEMENTARY LITERACY COACHES

January 2009

Literacy Coaching Clearinghouse

Name_____

I am answering the following self-assessment as an:

_____ Elementary School Literacy Coach

_____ Elementary School Reading Coach

_____ Elementary School Reading Specialist/Reading Teacher/Reading Support Teacher

_____ Elementary School Instructional Coach

The Self-Assessment for Elementary Literacy Coaches was adapted by the 2007–08 Literacy Coaching Clearinghouse Advisory Board from the Self-Assessment for Middle and High School Literacy Coaches.

Literacy Coach Standards Team Members who developed the original self-assessment were:

Doug Buehl, Madison Metropolitan School District, Madison, WI
Mark Conley, Michigan State University
Andres Henriques, Carnegie Corporation of New York
Jacy Ippolito, Graduate School of Education, Harvard University
Cathleen Kral, Boston Public Schools
Carlene Lodermeier, Iowa Department of Education Reading
Susan Pimentel, Standardswork
Cathy Roller, International Reading Association
Sharon Walpole, University of Delaware

(continued)

Criteria 1: Foundations of Literacy

Literacy coaches in elementary schools share with teachers an integrated body of research about how students become successful readers, writers, and communicators.

Please rate the following areas of knowledge using the rubric below:

Rubric:
1. I am not sufficiently knowledgeable about the topic, and need to learn more about it.
2. I am somewhat knowledgeable about the topic, BUT need to know more about current evidence-based practices and trends related to the topic.
3. I am knowledgeable about current evidence-based practices and trends related to the topic, BUT need to learn more about how to implement them.
4. I am knowledgeable about implementing current evidence-based practices and trends related to the topic, BUT need to learn how to communicate about such practices and trends to others.
5. I am experienced in implementing and sharing my knowledge of evidence-based practices and trends related to the topic in reading and/or writing blocks, BUT need to build my knowledge and skills about the topic across content areas.
6. I am experienced about implementing and sharing my knowledge of evidence-based practices and trends related to the topic in more than one content area, and am confident that I can apply similar skills in additional content areas.

Topics	Score (circle one)					
1. Developing students' oral language skills through discussion and dialogue	1	2	3	4	5	6
2. Developing students' speaking, listening, reading, and writing vocabularies	1	2	3	4	5	6
3. Developing connections among the language arts concerning how use of their interactive nature translates into good instruction	1	2	3	4	5	6
4. Developing students' text comprehension skills, (predicting, using prior knowledge, making inferences, drawing conclusions, retelling, and summarizing	1	2	3	4	5	6
5. Developing students' phonological awareness, including sensitivity to syllables, onsets and rimes, and phonemes	1	2	3	4	5	6

(continued)

SELF-ASSESSMENT FOR ELEMENTARY
LITERACY COACHES *(continued)*

Topics	Score (circle one)					
6. Developing students' letter-name and letter-sound knowledge	1	2	3	4	5	6
7. Developing students' ability to decode using sound-by-sound decoding and larger-unit decoding	1	2	3	4	5	6
8. Developing students' word identification skills including chunks, roots, bases, prefixes, suffixes, etc.	1	2	3	4	5	6
9. Developing students' store of words recognized automatically, by sight	1	2	3	4	5	6
10. Building students' reading fluency (including accuracy, rate, and expression) through extensive guided oral reading and means to monitor and provide corrective feedback	1	2	3	4	5	6
11. Developing students' meta-cognitive reading skills	1	2	3	4	5	6
12. Theories about literacy and the implications of low levels of literacy	1	2	3	4	5	6

After reviewing and reflecting on your answers above, please share (in a brief paragraph, bullets, or list) your thoughts about what you would like to know more about regarding this criteria in order to best serve your needs.

(continued)

SELF-ASSESSMENT FOR ELEMENTARY LITERACY COACHES *(continued)*

Criteria 2: Assessment

Literacy coaches in elementary schools lead faculty in understanding, selecting, and using multiple forms of assessments (including mandated external tests) as diagnostic tools to guide instructional decision-making and enhance both teacher and program effectiveness.

Please rate the following areas of knowledge using the rubric below:

Rubric:
1. I am not sufficiently knowledgeable about the topic, and need to learn more about it.
2. I am somewhat knowledgeable about the topic, BUT need to know more about current evidence-based practices and trends related to the topic.
3. I am knowledgeable about current evidence-based practices and trends related to the topic, BUT need to learn more about how to implement them.
4. I am knowledgeable about implementing current evidence-based practices and trends related to the topic, BUT need to learn how to communicate about such practices and trends to others.
5. I am experienced in implementing and sharing my knowledge of evidence-based practices and trends related to the topic in reading and/or writing blocks, BUT need to build my knowledge and skills about the topic across content areas.
6. I am experienced about implementing and sharing my knowledge of evidence-based practices and trends related to the topic in more than one content area, and am confident that I can apply similar skills in additional content areas.

Topics	Score (circle one)					
1. Determining whether a school's assessment system is coherent, comprehensive, and explicit	1	2	3	4	5	6
2. Implementing a coherent assessment system	1	2	3	4	5	6
3. Appropriate uses and interpretations of norm-referenced assessments	1	2	3	4	5	6
4. Appropriate uses and interpretations of criterion-referenced assessments	1	2	3	4	5	6
5. Appropriate uses and interpretations of informal assessments, such as teacher anecdotal records, student reflective journals, and student surveys	1	2	3	4	5	6
6. Appropriate uses and interpretations of formative assessments	1	2	3	4	5	6

(continued)

Topics	Score (circle one)					
7. Appropriate uses and interpretations of authentic assessments	1	2	3	4	5	6
8. Appropriate uses and interpretations of summative assessments	1	2	3	4	5	6
9. Appropriate uses and interpretations of commercial program assessments	1	2	3	4	5	6
10. Appropriate uses and interpretations of diagnostic or screening assessments to identify students' specific literacy strengths and needs	1	2	3	4	5	6
11. Appropriate uses and interpretations of state-mandated assessments	1	2	3	4	5	6
12. Appropriate uses and interpretations of assessment data to inform and improve professional development efforts	1	2	3	4	5	6
13. Appropriate uses and interpretations of assessments to provide teachers with information to differentiate instruction in order to meet the needs of diverse classroom populations	1	2	3	4	5	6
14. Monitoring the effectiveness of a school's literacy improvement action plan, including a review of achievement data, surveys of faculty and other stakeholders, and observations of teachers implementing new literacy strategies	1	2	3	4	5	6
15. Assessing and understanding the role in instruction of students' individual interests, backgrounds, cultures, reading histories, and writing histories	1	2	3	4	5	6
16. Communicating the goals and results of various assessments to different audiences at the school and district levels for their reflection and action, including teachers, administrators, students, and parents	1	2	3	4	5	6

After reviewing and reflecting on your answers above, please share (in a brief paragraph, bullets, or list) your thoughts about what you would like to know more about regarding this criteria in order to best serve your needs.

(continued)

Criteria 3: Content Area Instruction

Literacy coaches in elementary school assist teachers in understanding how they can develop students' knowledge and related skills while simultaneously improving student reading and learning in specific content areas (e.g., Social Studies, Language Arts, Math, Science, etc.).

Please rate the following areas of knowledge using the rubric below:

Rubric:
1. I am not sufficiently knowledgeable about the topic, and need to learn more about it.
2. I am somewhat knowledgeable about the topic, BUT need to know more about current evidence-based practices and trends related to the topic.
3. I am knowledgeable about current evidence-based practices and trends related to the topic, BUT need to learn more about how to implement them.
4. I am knowledgeable about implementing current evidence-based practices and trends related to the topic, BUT need to learn how to communicate about such practices and trends to others.
5. I am experienced in implementing and sharing my knowledge of evidence-based practices and trends related to the topic in reading and/or writing blocks, BUT need to build my knowledge and skills about the topic across content areas.
6. I am experienced about implementing and sharing my knowledge of evidence-based practices and trends related to the topic in more than one content area, and am confident that I can apply similar skills in additional content areas.

Topics	Score (circle one)					
1. Content area/discipline-specific student standards, benchmarks and goals (content, skills, and dispositions)	1	2	3	4	5	6
2. Content area/discipline-specific understanding of foundational literacy (including vocabulary, comprehension, and fluency); adjustment of rate depending on purpose and on type of text	1	2	3	4	5	6
3. Content area/Discipline-specific cognitive strategies to promote literacy and develop active and competent learners in the core content areas	1	2	3	4	5	6

(continued)

Topics	Score (circle one)					
4. Knowledge of ways to use writing to think through understanding of a content area/discipline; combining reading with writing or other forms of multimodal forms of representation	1	2	3	4	5	6
5. Content area/discipline-specific methodologies of communicating and representing content	1	2	3	4	5	6
6. Content area/discipline-specific teaching practices that promote the development of multiple comprehension strategies	1	2	3	4	5	6
7. Content area/discipline-specific texts at a variety of reading levels	1	2	3	4	5	6
8. Engagement of students in problem solving methodologies through dialogue, discussion, project-based learning, and group work	1	2	3	4	5	6
9. Analysis and selection of content area/discipline-specific resources that supplement print texts, including video, digital media, visual media, etc.	1	2	3	4	5	6
10. Content area/discipline-specific assessment practices	1	2	3	4	5	6

After reviewing and reflecting on your answers above, please share (in a brief paragraph, bullets, or list) your thoughts about what you would like to know more about regarding this criteria in order to best serve your needs.

(continued)

Criteria 4: Writing

Literacy coaches in elementary school assist teachers in understanding how they can develop students' writing.

Please rate the following areas of knowledge using the rubric below:

Rubric:
1. I am not sufficiently knowledgeable about the topic, and need to learn more about it.
2. I am somewhat knowledgeable about the topic, BUT need to know more about current evidence-based practices and trends related to the topic.
3. I am knowledgeable about current evidence-based practices and trends related to the topic, BUT need to learn more about how to implement them.
4. I am knowledgeable about implementing current evidence-based practices and trends related to the topic, BUT need to learn how to communicate about such practices and trends to others.
5. I am experienced in implementing and sharing my knowledge of evidence-based practices and trends related to the topic in reading and/or writing blocks, BUT need to build my knowledge and skills about the topic across content areas.
6. I am experienced about implementing and sharing my knowledge of evidence-based practices and trends related to the topic in more than one content area, and am confident that I can apply similar skills in additional content areas.

Topics	Score (circle one)					
1. Knowledgeable of ways to develop students' writing skills through scaffolded instruction and assignments	1	2	3	4	5	6
2. Knowledgeable of a wide range of genres of writing	1	2	3	4	5	6
3. Knowledgeable of strategies to differentiate writing instruction for a wide range of learners	1	2	3	4	5	6
4. Knowledgeable of ways to help students revise drafts for content	1	2	3	4	5	6
5. Knowledgeable of ways to help students edit for mechanical errors	1	2	3	4	5	6
6. Knowledgeable of ways to help students develop ideas, organization, content, and voice	1	2	3	4	5	6

(continued)

Topics	Score (circle one)					
7. Knowledgeable of ways to help students develop and improve their grammar, spelling, capitalization, and punctuation	1	2	3	4	5	6
8. Knowledgeable of ways to assess writing processes and products	1	2	3	4	5	6
9. Knowledgeable of various ways to motivate reluctant writers	1	2	3	4	5	6
10. Knowledgeable of ways that technology can assist students' development of sound writing processes and production of final products	1	2	3	4	5	6
11. Knowledgeable of software and other technology applications that would help students develop their abilities as writers	1	2	3	4	5	6

After reviewing and reflecting on your answers above, please share (in a brief paragraph, bullets, or list) your thoughts about what you would like to know more about regarding this criteria in order to best serve your needs.

(continued)

Criteria 5: Differentiated Instruction

Literacy coaches work with elementary teachers to support the development and implementation of differentiated instruction to serve the needs of the full range of learners in their classrooms.

Please rate the following areas of knowledge using the rubric below:

Rubric:
1. I am not sufficiently knowledgeable about the topic, and need to learn more about it.
2. I am somewhat knowledgeable about the topic, BUT need to know more about current evidence-based practices and trends related to the topic.
3. I am knowledgeable about current evidence-based practices and trends related to the topic, BUT need to learn more about how to implement them.
4. I am knowledgeable about implementing current evidence-based practices and trends related to the topic, BUT need to learn how to communicate about such practices and trends to others.
5. I am experienced in implementing and sharing my knowledge of evidence-based practices and trends related to the topic in reading and/or writing blocks, BUT need to build my knowledge and skills about the topic across content areas.
6. I am experienced about implementing and sharing my knowledge of evidence-based practices and trends related to the topic in more than one content area, and am confident that I can apply similar skills in additional content areas.

Topics	Score (circle one)					
1. Interpreting diagnostic tools used to differentiate instruction and adapt to individual student needs	1	2	3	4	5	6
2. Multiple classroom strategies and instructional practices that scaffold learning for a classroom of diverse learners	1	2	3	4	5	6
3. Differentiating literacy content, process/assignment task, and product to meet the needs of a diverse classroom population—from struggling to highly proficient readers	1	2	3	4	5	6
4. Flexible classroom grouping structures (including partner shares, cooperative groups, project teams, re-teaching arrangements, and tutoring supports)	1	2	3	4	5	6

(continued)

Topics	Score (circle one)					
5. Knowledge of effective instructional practices to reach gifted and talented readers in content area classes	1	2	3	4	5	6
6. Knowledge of effective instructional practices to reach students with learning disabilities related to literacy	1	2	3	4	5	6
7. Knowledge of effective instructional practices to reach English Language Learners	1	2	3	4	5	6
8. Analysis and selection of text materials that meet the needs of a diverse classroom population—from struggling to highly proficient readers	1	2	3	4	5	6
9. Analysis and selection of curriculum materials that reflect the diversity of a multicultural classroom population	1	2	3	4	5	6
10. Building classroom libraries that represent a variety of genres and interests and link to multiple reading levels	1	2	3	4	5	6

After reviewing and reflecting on your answers above, please share (in a brief paragraph, bullets, or list) your thoughts about what you would like to know more about regarding this criteria in order to best serve your needs.

(continued)

SELF-ASSESSMENT FOR ELEMENTARY
LITERACY COACHES *(continued)*

Criteria 6: Classroom Coaching
(Working One-on-One With Teachers)

Literacy coaches work with teachers individually to emphasize best practices in the areas of curricula, literacy skills, and teacher attitudes, while providing practical support on a full range of reading, writing, and communication strategies to increase student achievement.

Please rate the following areas of knowledge using the rubric below:

Rubric
1. I am not sufficiently knowledgeable about the topic, and need to learn more about it.
2. I am somewhat knowledgeable about the topic, BUT need to know more about current evidence-based practices and trends related to the topic.
3. I am knowledgeable about current evidence-based practices and trends related to the topic, BUT need to learn more about how to implement them.
4. I am knowledgeable about implementing current evidence-based practices and trends related to the topic, BUT need to learn how to communicate about such practices and trends to others.
5. I am experienced in implementing and sharing my knowledge of evidence-based practices and trends related to the topic in reading and/or writing blocks, BUT need to build my knowledge and skills about the topic across content areas.
6. I am experienced about implementing and sharing my knowledge of evidence-based practices and trends related to the topic in more than one content area, and am confident that I can apply similar skills in additional content areas.

Topics	Score (circle one)					
1. "Over-the-shoulder" coaching (i.e., coaching in the moment and providing teacher support during instruction)	1	2	3	4	5	6
2. Collaborative planning (i.e., goals, units, lessons, assessments)	1	2	3	4	5	6
3. "Gradual release" model of coaching	1	2	3	4	5	6
4. Observation practices (i.e., planning, pre-meeting, observation protocols, video-taping, and reflective dialogues)	1	2	3	4	5	6
5. Modeling and demonstrating classroom lessons	1	2	3	4	5	6
6. Effective co-teaching/team teaching	1	2	3	4	5	6

(continued)

Topics	Score (circle one)					
7. Establishing classroom routines and management structures	1	2	3	4	5	6
8. Facilitating the effective collection and analysis of student data to organize instruction	1	2	3	4	5	6
9. Ongoing collection of data on the impact of the one-on-one classroom coaching	1	2	3	4	5	6
10. Defining/clarifying role and relationship with administrator and teachers	1	2	3	4	5	6

After reviewing and reflecting on your answers above, please share (in a brief paragraph, bullets, or list) your thoughts about what you would like to know more about regarding this criteria in order to best serve your needs.

(continued)

SELF-ASSESSMENT FOR ELEMENTARY
LITERACY COACHES *(continued)*

Criteria 7: Facilitating Adult Learning

Literacy coaches bring fresh perspectives and experiences to helping teachers and other adults in the school system break through barriers that inhibit student achievement.

Please rate the following areas of knowledge using the rubric below:

Rubric
1. I am not sufficiently knowledgeable about the topic, and need to learn more about it.
2. I am somewhat knowledgeable about the topic, BUT need to know more about current evidence-based practices and trends related to the topic.
3. I am knowledgeable about current evidence-based practices and trends related to the topic, BUT need to learn more about how to implement them.
4. I am knowledgeable about implementing current evidence-based practices and trends related to the topic, BUT need to learn how to communicate about such practices and trends to others.
5. I am experienced in implementing and sharing my knowledge of evidence-based practices and trends related to the topic.

Topics	Score (circle one)				
1. Theories in adult development, learning, and motivation in order to meet the needs of school staff members at different stages in their careers	1	2	3	4	5
2. Theories related to quality professional development aimed at accelerating student learning	1	2	3	4	5
3. Adult learning processes that lead to improved instructional practices, reflective practitioners, and expertise in meta-cognitive reading strategies	1	2	3	4	5
4. Asset-based learning that focuses on teachers' strengths	1	2	3	4	5
5. Facilitating change in the face of resistance (e.g., managing difficult conversations, negotiating win-win situations)	1	2	3	4	5

(continued)

Topics	Score (circle one)				
6. Supporting adult learning (e.g. communicating respect, safeguarding confidentiality, offering planning time, teaching about stress management, providing incentives)	1	2	3	4	5
7. Facilitating varied group configurations and presentation formats (whole staff, departmental, and small group training)	1	2	3	4	5
8. Gathering, collecting, and analyzing information related to the level of implementation of the targeted instructional practices (including fidelity to the practice)	1	2	3	4	5

After reviewing and reflecting on your answers above, please share (in a brief paragraph, bullets, or list) your thoughts about what you would like to know more about regarding this criteria in order to best serve your needs.

(continued)

Criteria 8: Building Capacity Within the School

Literacy coaches serve as catalysts for reform by engaging all stakeholders of the school community in the design and implementation of effective processes that lead to enduring changes in the school culture.

Please rate the following areas of knowledge using the rubric below:

Rubric
1. I am not sufficiently knowledgeable about the topic, and need to learn more about it.
2. I am somewhat knowledgeable about the topic, BUT need to know more about current evidence-based practices and trends related to the topic.
3. I am knowledgeable about current evidence-based practices and trends related to the topic, BUT need to learn more about how to implement them.
4. I am knowledgeable about implementing current evidence-based practices and trends related to the topic, BUT need to learn how to communicate about such practices and trends to others.
5. I am experienced in implementing and sharing my knowledge of evidence-based practices and trends related to the topic.

Topics	Score (circle one)				
1. Assessing schoolwide literacy needs	1	2	3	4	5
2. Establishing a school literacy team to oversee the development and implementation of a literacy improvement action plan	1	2	3	4	5
3. Determining key elements of a schoolwide literacy program	1	2	3	4	5
4. Effectively implementing a schoolwide literacy program	1	2	3	4	5
5. Monitoring a schoolwide literacy program for level of implementation and effectiveness	1	2	3	4	5
6. Communicating about schoolwide literacy program to staff, administration, departments, and other stakeholders	1	2	3	4	5
7. Coordinating efforts between staff, administration, departments, and other stakeholders regarding schoolwide literacy program (e.g., working effectively with literacy and leadership teams)	1	2	3	4	5

(continued)

Topics	Score (circle one)				
8. Problem solving "barriers" that may impede the effectiveness of the literacy program	1	2	3	4	5
9. Mentoring building administrators in coaching strategies and effective literacy practices	1	2	3	4	5
10. Coordinating coaching efforts with other classroom support specialists (e.g., ELL, LD, department chairs, etc.)	1	2	3	4	5
11. Strategies to "scale-up" the adoption of new literacy instructional practices in schools	1	2	3	4	5
12. Sustaining new literacy instructional practices	1	2	3	4	5
13. Integrating technology into the life of the school, (including classroom instruction	1	2	3	4	5

After reviewing and reflecting on your answers above, please share (in a brief paragraph, bullets, or list) your thoughts about what you would like to know more about regarding this criteria in order to best serve your needs.

(continued)

SELF-ASSESSMENT FOR ELEMENTARY
LITERACY COACHES *(continued)*

**Criteria 9: Working Within a Broader
School Reform Context**

Literacy coaches are knowledgeable advocates for the implementation of effective school reform practices and comprehensive and coordinated literacy programs that have a positive impact on student performance nationally.

Please rate the following areas of knowledge using the rubric below:

Rubric:
1. I am not sufficiently knowledgeable about the topic, and need to learn more about it.
2. I am somewhat knowledgeable about the topic, BUT need to know more about current evidence-based practices and trends related to the topic.
3. I am knowledgeable about current evidence-based practices and trends related to the topic, BUT need to learn more about how to implement them.
4. I am knowledgeable about implementing current evidence-based practices and trends related to the topic, BUT need to learn how to communicate about such practices and trends to others.
5. I am experienced in implementing and sharing my knowledge of evidence-based practices and trends related to the topic.

Topics	Score (circle one)				
1. Principles of effective school reform (e.g., standards, accountability, communities of practice or lesson study)	1	2	3	4	5
2. Implementing school schedules and structures that support literacy instructional practices across content areas within the broader context of school reform	1	2	3	4	5
3. Coordinating school reform concepts in the context of federal, state, and district mandates (NCLB, RTI, Title I, ELL, grant programs, special education, etc.)	1	2	3	4	5
4. Building connections with the local community	1	2	3	4	5

(continued)

Topics	Score (circle one)
5. Addressing barriers that can impede effective school reform	1 2 3 4 5

After reviewing and reflecting on your answers above, please share (in a brief paragraph, bullets, or list) your thoughts about what you would like to know more about regarding this criteria in order to best serve your needs.

Practical Literacy Coaching: A Collection of Tools to Support Your Work by Jan Miller Burkins.
© 2009 International Reading Association. May be copied for classroom use.

A Coaching Story:
Reading With a Different Lens

Because many coaches are quite isolated, the tools in this chapter are designed to help coaches support themselves and, in some cases, to support each other. While the support available for coaches has dramatically increased since I began coaching six years ago, the dearth of resources and professional opportunities for literacy coaches in my early coaching days led me to be creative in the ways I supported my own professional growth.

Quite by accident, I discovered that if I read a book about teaching or watched a video from the perspective of a coach rather than that of a teacher, I could dramatically increase the scope of resources to which I had access. By engaging this shift in perspective, I stumbled upon some learning that prompted me to write *Coaching for Balance*. For example, I was reading *The Art of Teaching Writing* by Lucy Calkins (1994) when I realized that much of what she suggested for teachers holding conferences with students was directly translatable to my work with teachers.

This "aha" has been powerful for my growth as a coach. Basically, any book or video about teaching can be read from the perspective of a literacy coach who works with teachers. Watching video footage of teachers holding conferences with students has had a profound impact on the ways I communicate with teachers. In fact, some of the language of suggestion that I access the most comes from a video called *Inside Reading and Writing Workshops* (Hindley, 1998), which shows Joanne Hindley conferring with readers.

So, if you need a professional vitamin, particularly if you are not tapped into a network of coaches or in a district that is thoughtful and systematic about your professional learning, I suggest rereading books you have that relate to aspects of your work. For example, books on conferring with students about reading and writing, on the language of classroom instruction, on asking better questions, or on promoting student reflection are likely to translate into your coaching practice.

Coaching Connection:
Yoga and Honoring Resistance

This chapter has been about your practice of stretching yourself professionally. My experience with personal stretching has informed my thinking along these lines. I have a yoga DVD I use sometimes to support my random and intermittent practice of yoga approximations. As I was beginning to start the DVD one night, I asked my husband if he would like to try it with me. He responded without hesitation, "I'll snap in half!" His comment made me laugh out loud. (Even as I record his statement here, the idea strikes me as funny.) Contrary to the mental image conjured by the idea of a person over bending and snapping, there is something about the gentle, consistent pressure of yoga that, over time, causes us to change. And there is something valuable in honoring the resistance of your body.

Such is the nature of the reflective work we practice. Generally, it is most beneficial as gentle, consistent pressure that translates into strength and flexibility developed over time. Other times, our progress is dramatic. There have been times when my professional learning has been so great and so fast that I thought I would snap in half. Katie Wood Ray (1999) writes that she has gone through periods of such intense learning that she emerges from it a different person. I have experienced this, too. On the other hand, I have worked through repeated exercises that have gently shaped my practice, little by little, in big ways. The growth trajectories we experience will vary with spurts and plateaus. I encourage you to honor your own resistance and focus on working courageously and consistently.

Resources for Stretching Yourself

1. In *Differentiated Literacy Coaching: Scaffolding for Student and Teacher Success*, Mary Catherine Moran (2007) offers 13 role-play vignettes for literacy coaches and 12 professional learning modules. These are great for literacy coaches to work through together and support each other's professional learning.

2. If you are examining the language of your coaching (and perhaps even your life), there are two books you must read:

   a. With poetic and passionate style, Peter Johnston (2004) delicately analyzes the common language of classroom instruction in *Choice Words: How Our Language Affects Children's Learning*. While the book is written with an audience of teachers in mind, the connections to coaching are clear and valuable. No other book has more appreciably influenced the way I work with teachers.

   b. In *Fierce Conversations: Achieving Success at Work and in Life, One Conversation at a Time*, Susan Scott (2002) energetically shares her experience from the corporate world where she counsels people on how to improve communication skills. While the topic is not new, Scott's use of language and her willingness to be direct with the reader make the book engaging, and her practical suggestions make it immediately applicable. I think I highlighted the whole thing!

Taking Chapter 3 Personally:
How Are You Stretching *Your*self?

Questions for Reflection

• What outside sources—whether people or texts—can you count on to honestly stretch you and your work beyond your biases and the paradigms you have adopted to frame your work as a literacy coach?

• What are your professional goals for this year? Why?

• How are you systematically attending to your own professional growth? How have you enlisted the support of your school and district administrations?

Possible Action Steps

• Connect with another literacy coach and make a commitment to support each other professionally. Develop a calendar that details the monthly work you will complete to help one another stretch. Plug some of the tools in this section into that calendar.

• Locate a professional resource that addresses reading or writing conferences in classrooms. Read the book through the lens of a literacy coach. Share what you learn with a colleague.

• Visit the Literacy Coaching Clearinghouse (www.literacycoachingonline .org) and complete the literacy coach self-assessment most relevant to you. Identify an area of growth for yourself. Also read the reviews of coaching texts. Locate one that will support the area you have targeted for professional stretching.

CHAPTER 4

Developing and Supporting Learning Communities

"Learning is not compulsory...neither is survival."
William H. Deming

Opening Thoughts: Smart Work

I have been in many meetings, usually where people who are not regularly in classrooms are deciding on additional responsibilities for teachers. The facilitator emphatically states, "We don't need to work harder; we need to work smarter." More often than not, the "smarter, not harder" cliché excuses those who are exponentially increasing the responsibilities of already overburdened teachers. However, there is one context I have found where there really are some ways to work smarter to lighten your workload: that is in planning professional learning.

Over the course of the last 10 years, my philosophy of teaching adults has evolved as I have worked in school districts, taught graduate classes, and facilitated professional learning at our school. Here are a couple of ideas related to supporting the learning community within your school, all of which represent ways that we can "work smarter" to affect classroom instruction.

First, model what you want to see in classrooms. You can't, for example, facilitate a professional learning session around higher order thinking and deliver it through a lecture and a PowerPoint presentation. If you want teachers to engage students, you have to show them how by first engaging them. If you want teachers to differentiate for student learning, then you have to differentiate for the levels of understanding represented in the faculty of your school. If you want teachers to scaffold student learning through the Gradual Release of Responsibility Model, then you must do the same for them.

Second, provide opportunities for teachers to engage in dialogue and support their inquiry. That is, let teachers arrive at their own understandings. There are some things that are factual in the area of literacy, but much of teaching is gray. The understandings at which teachers arrive on their own are usually better understood and better learned than those that we presume to hand them. As indicated earlier, facilitating "inquiry" learning when you already have *the* right answer (or at least feel as if you do) is manipulation rather than inquiry. However, inquiry where you have some general understandings you would like to support but where you are open to the conclusions to which the teachers arrive themselves is more sincere and generally more effective. Again, supporting inquiry and dialogue usually takes less preparation and lends itself to deeper learning, thus we are again working smarter.

Third, invite collaboration. Robert Eaker, Richard DuFour, and Rebecca DuFour (2002) write, "Schools that function as professional learning communities are always characterized by a collaborative culture. Teacher isolation is replaced with collaborative processes that are deeply embedded into the daily life of the school" (p. 5). The more the teachers in your school can support, teach, and encourage one another, the more they will not only acquire new, discrete skills but will also simply become better at learning.

These three relatively simple ideas can revolutionize the professional learning in your school. However, behind their simplicity lies a series of complex decisions for the literacy coach. Which protocol do I use and when? Is this content best shared in a small- or large-group context? How do I follow up with teachers? What types of scaffolding do individual teachers need? This chapter offers you support in negotiating some of these decisions.

Coaching Connection: Red Grapes or Green Grapes

Recently, after a gruelingly long day of literacy coaching, I came home obviously exhausted. My husband offered to get me a snack, adding that he had just purchased a bunch of grapes. I collapsed on the couch and nodded affirmatively in regard to the grapes. Then he asked, "Would you like red or green grapes? We have both." Apparently, this simple question was the one just over the limits of my decision-making threshold, because I suddenly burst out crying. There have been similar days when questions like "Paper or plastic?" were so cognitively demanding in the wake of the myriad of decisions that fill my day as a coach that I find myself shutting down completely.

I have read research on how many decisions a teacher makes in a given day. A doctoral student in search of an interesting dissertation should conduct similar research on the array and the diversity of decisions that face literacy coaches. Because the sheer vastness and comprehensiveness of the decision making inherent in coaching can be overwhelming, tools that assist us in strategically making these decisions or in prioritizing the areas that exercise our decision-making muscles can offer coaches some sorely needed relief.

Related Research: Learning to Learn

One way that a literacy coach can become more productive is by giving teachers opportunities to become more efficient in the ways they learn. The previously mentioned research of Joyce and Showers (2002) demonstrates that teachers can become more effective professional learners if they are in learning environments that support them in certain ways. Primarily, such teachers are involved in collaborative learning environments or professional learning communities. They write,

> Both anecdotal and interview data indicate that the effects of coaching are much more far reaching than the mastery and integration of new knowledge and skills by individual teachers. The development of school norms that support the continuous study and improvement of teaching apparently build capability for other kinds of change, whether it is adoption of a new curriculum, a school wide discipline policy, or the building of teaching repertoire. (p. 82)

Thus, the energy you invest in establishing norms of collegiality and professionalism offers benefits beyond the specific skill or content you are exploring with teachers. Some work in the area of developing learning communities will lead to more and better work in other areas and poises teachers to be more receptive of and more efficient in other learning situations. Joyce and Showers go on to speak of this as a "'learning to learn' aptitude" (p. 77), something that literacy coaches relish in a school community.

Tools for Developing and Supporting Learning Communities

Orientation to Tool 15:
Phases of Learning Reflection Form

Jennifer Allen (2006) writes, "one of my most important jobs is to plan my time well" (p. 138). The first tool in this section is specifically designed to support you as you study the learning needs of the teachers in your school in an effort to concentrate your energies in the places where patterns of need emerge and to "plan your time well." The Phases of

Learning Reflection Form is a reflective lens through which you can consider individually and collectively the places of learning that your teachers presently inhabit. The purpose of the form is simply to help coaches consider where to invest their time and how to effectively plan differentiated professional learning support for teachers. In addition, the Phases of Learning Reflection Form can help coaches consider their own learning histories and the areas in which specific learning formats have resulted in varying levels of teacher learning and growth.

The intent of this tool is not to pigeonhole teachers into categories or to "evaluate" teachers but rather to help coaches organize their thoughts and reflections in an effort to identify patterns across the school and manage valuable professional learning time with teachers. The end results, hopefully, will be more teachers reaching a higher level of skill because coaches are considering the individual needs of teachers and maximizing their coaching efforts. As a modification of the form, you could explain the phases of learning to teachers and ask them to share where they feel they are and what support they need.

LINK TO COACHING FOR BALANCE

For a complete description of the phases of learning, see Table 2, "Comparison of Phases of Learning," on page 108.

PHASES OF LEARNING REFLECTION FORM

Area of focus_____ Date_____

Teacher	Initiating	Clarifying	Cultivating	Integrating	Inventing	Nature of support from coach/action steps

PHASES OF LEARNING REFLECTION FORM SAMPLE

Area of focus_____*Guided Reading*_____ Date_*November 12, 2008*_

Teacher	Initiating	Clarifying	Cultivating	Integrating	Inventing	Nature of support from coach/action steps
Smith	X					New to school--needs initial professional learning in guided reading
Jones			X			Seems to understand-- get into her classroom and watch her teach to clarify any misunderstandings before they are habituated
Sampson					X	Schedule time for other teachers to observe in his room
Massey		X				Has requested a meeting time after school to talk through questions that have arisen after initial efforts to implement
McGuire	X					New to school--needs initial professional learning in guided reading
Brindle	X					Has had initial professional learning but never really implemented; has expressed renewed interest--may want to sit in if there is professional learning for Smith and McGuire; get her a copy of professional text to read
Caldwell					X	Schedule time for other teachers to observe in his room
Jenkins			X			Has expressed some confusion over ways to support word solving; relies heavily on directing children to decode. I am scheduled to meet with her to practice, need to schedule demonstration lessons
Williams				X		Visit classroom to support and encourage; meet with teacher to decide next area of exploration

Orientation to Tool 16: Ten Ways to Mix Groups

In facilitating professional learning, it is not uncommon for the groups with whom you are working to fall into the comfortable rhythms of interacting with those most familiar to them. Faculties tend to cluster around grade-level groups or into groups of people who share common philosophies. This can interfere with a literacy coach's efforts to promote new thinking or to support shifts from less productive paradigms. It can, on a more elemental level, also create management difficulties as social groups are more likely to engage in tangential conversation, to assume they already understand each other, and to take shortcuts in the work. Because of this, literacy coaches can explore the effects of shuffling groups.

Mixing the groups within a faculty can be surprisingly challenging. When I was a language arts consultant for the state, we tried setting the materials out in the places we wanted teachers to sit, but they still moved them and sat where they were comfortable. We would only put chairs around certain tables, but teachers would move them to remain in their groups, even if this meant there were twice as many teachers at one table.

Mixing the arrangement of the participants in a professional learning situation is likely to invite moans and groans. However, I encourage you to try it because the payoff in the learning is worth the invested effort. Furthermore, once teachers get accustomed to stepping out of their comfort zones, they will hesitate less and less.

Daphne Hall, an instructional coach in my school district, and I were charged with mixing our professional coaches group each week for our district professional learning. We found it surprisingly challenging. To save you some time, I am including this list of 10 strategies for mixing up groups of people who otherwise would tend to gather around predictable social structures. You also can refer to the teampedia website (www.teampedia .net) for more ideas about how to get people to interact with one another in new ways.

TEN WAYS TO MIX GROUPS

1. The Birthday Method: Label each table with months and ask teachers to sit according to their birthdays. Note: This will give you uneven groups. As a variation, have teachers sit in order of their birthdays. This requires a lot of conversation and people with birthdays close together get to connect.

2. The Highlighter Method: Label each table with a color and highlight names on the sign-in sheet. Teachers need to sit according to the color in which their name is highlighted.

3. The Elementary Recess Method: Have teachers number off and move into groups according to number. This is most effective when people shuffle after everyone has arrived for the meeting.

4. The Crayon Method: Distribute crayons from boxes of 8 crayons (or 12 or 24, depending on how many groups you want). Ask teachers to sit at a table with others with the same color crayon. You can vary this by using boxes of 12, 16, or 24 crayons. The number of crayons represents the number of groups that will form.

5. The M & M Method: Repeat the crayon method, but use M & Ms or some sort of colored candy. The facilitator must make sure there are even numbers of each color before distributing the M&Ms, otherwise group sizes will vary.

6. The Musical Chairs Method: Once participants are seated, ask them to get up and visit with their colleagues at other tables. Tell them that when the music starts, they are to sit down immediately at the chair closest to them. Once they find a new place to sit, they will have to go back and get their materials. Moving quickly keeps people from working to figure out how to stay with those with whom they are most comfortable.

7. The Colored Sticky Note Method: Stick a different colored sticky note on the back of or underneath each chair. Use as many different colors as you have tables. Once participants are seated, have them look at the sticky note on their chair and move to the group formed by that particular sticky note color.

8. The Fruit Basket Turnover: At each table, place enough of one kind of fruit for everyone to have a piece (people are likely to sit at a table that has a fruit they like). Once everyone is seated, have them take their piece of fruit and move to a table where each piece of fruit is represented, thus creating a "fruit basket." Then they can eat their fruit. This is a rather expensive method, but if you are planning to provide refreshments, this is a healthy, fun alternative.

9. The Flower Arrangement: Repeat the Fruit Basket Turnover but use flowers. When the mixed groups are assembled, the flowers are placed in a vase. Names can be drawn to see who takes home the flower arrangements as a door prize.

10. The Name Tag Method: Make name tags for participants. Code each name tag by color or with stickers. Ask teachers to sit with others with the same code on their name tag.

Practical Literacy Coaching: A Collection of Tools to Support Your Work by Jan Miller Burkins.
© 2009 International Reading Association. May be copied for classroom use.

Orientation to Tools 17–18:
Teacher Self-Assessments

Because they develop professional learning capacities and encourage teacher reflection, I have found self-assessments to be a tremendous tool for teacher growth. While a self-assessment can help teachers examine their practice within a particular area of instruction and serve as a way for a literacy coach to identify patterns of need throughout a school, they also serve as a teaching tool. By describing the various aspects of instruction around or within literacy, a well-developed self-assessment serves as a guide for making instructional change.

I have used self-assessments with teachers since the very beginning of my work as a literacy coach. I typically give teachers time to work through the self-assessment at the beginning of the school year and then again at the end of the year so that teachers set goals and then review their progress. I have not always collected these but have used them as both an opportunity for private reflection for teachers and as a needs assessment for me. By simply reviewing the self-assessment form with teachers, a coach can quickly review critical elements of instruction. In my experience, teachers respond quite positively to this nonthreatening way of documenting their professional growth and narrowing their learning focus.

The two self-assessment instruments that follow vary in format and content. One is general with a few specific details offered in each area of a literacy framework, while the other looks more closely at guided reading, one area of an overall literacy framework. I share them both with you to give you a sense of the variety of possibilities for using self-assessments.

The Literacy Framework Self-Assessment was developed by Kim Cox, Cathy Crable, and Jean Stein, who work in the Wayne Central School District in Ontario Center, New York, USA. One thing I like about this particular self-assessment is that it asks teachers to record both quantitative (a numeric rating) and qualitative (a written reflection) responses to each area.

Susan Trask, from Auburn School District in Auburn, ME, USA, contributed the Guided Reading Self-Assessment, which illustrates how a self-assessment might be used to look at a specific area of literacy instruction. There are a number of guided reading self-assessments available, and I received several when I solicited submissions for this book. What I like about this one is that it is simple; some self-assessments can focus too intently on details and overwhelm teachers.

LITERACY FRAMEWORK SELF-ASSESSMENT

Date:	Teacher:
1 = I am just beginning to explore this element and need support in getting started. 3 = I have engaged in some work in this area but need support in refining my efforts. 5 = I am confident about my work in this area and could support other teachers as they initiate similar work.	
<u>Self-selected reading</u> My multilevel independent reading time includes • A wide variety of literature • Student choice • Focus on reading interest • Motivation for reading • Response to reading through journaling or conferences • Independent reading level • Documentation and conferences	_____Reflection:
<u>Guided reading</u> My lesson includes before-, during-, and after-reading elements. My lesson has a clear focus. I place students in flexible groups to address interests, ability, or skill development. • <u>Before:</u> Developing prior knowledge through picture walks, vocabulary building, making predictions, K-W-L, connection to prior experiences, setting purpose • <u>During:</u> Using strategies, developing fluency, developing comprehension, developing vocabulary, studying genre traits, building motivation, supporting student reading practice • <u>After:</u> Building connections between new learning and previous learning, following up on predictions, reflecting metacognitively on new reading skills and strategies	_____Reflection:

(continued)

Practical Literacy Coaching: A Collection of Tools to Support Your Work by Jan Miller Burkins.
© 2009 International Reading Association. May be copied for classroom use.

Read-aloud
I model fluent, expressive, and phrased reading of text. I often include "think-aloud" strategies for making text connections, asking questions, making predictions, and using prior knowledge. I read aloud in a variety of settings: whole group, small group, and with individuals, and I include
  • A variety of genres
  • Fiction and nonfiction
  • Challenging and engaging text
	_____Reflection:

Word work
I include reading and spelling of high-frequency words. Students begin by learning a new skill with me and then at a center/station they continue to develop the skill through targeted activities. These activities are multilevel and targeted to student strengths and needs.
  • Spelling patterns
  • Word walls or star words
  • Writing, chanting, singing, peer work
  • Self-correcting
  • Rhyming, word sorts, concentration games
  • Support for vocabulary development
	_____Reflection:

Writing
I include both student-selected and teacher-directed writing opportunities. The writing block contains a minilesson where I target a trait, a skill, or a genre of writing and then I provide opportunities to practice or refine this skill in an authentic piece of writing.
  • Minilesson
  • Individual targets
  • Student choice
  • Writing process
  • Peer editing
  • Teacher conferences and documentation
	_____Reflection:

Created by Kim Cox, Cathy Crable, and Jean Stein.

GUIDED READING SELF-ASSESSMENT

Directions: For each category, circle the box that represents your present level of implementation, with "1" representing the simplest level of implementation and "4" representing the most complex.

	1	2	3	4
Grouping	• My groups remain the same all year. • Tested reading level is the only criterion I use to form groups.	• My group configurations rarely change. • Tested reading level may be the only criterion I use to form groups.	• My group configurations change occasionally. • Tested reading level may be the only criterion I use to form groups.	• My groups are in flexible configurations, which change often. • I use a variety of data to form groups (benchmarking, observations, student interests, etc.).
Text selection	• I choose books on the basis of the reading level alone. • I engage in little or no analysis of the text's challenges and supportive features.	• I choose books on the basis of the reading level alone. • I engage in basic analysis of the text's challenges and supportive features.	• I choose books on the basis of one or two criteria. • I engage in basic analysis of the text's challenges and supportive features.	• I choose books based on interests, skills, curriculum, and text features. • I engage in a thorough analysis of text challenges and supports in order to strategically plan my lesson.

(continued)

GUIDED READING SELF-ASSESSMENT
(continued)

	1	**2**	**3**	**4**
Lesson focus and instruction	• I do not include strategy instruction in the lesson. • I do not introduce the reading selection at all.	• I mention reading strategies, but I do not emphasize them during the lesson. • I include a minimal introduction of the reading selection.	• My lessons include a major focus on strategic reading (i.e., strategies readers use). • I generally introduce the reading selection in order to narrow its challenges.	• My lessons include a major focus on strategic reading and a reflection on the strategies at the end. • I carefully introduce selections to scaffold student learning.
Analysis	• I do not analyze student strategy use. • I do not "check in" with, or listen to, students as they read.	• I try to analyze student strategy use, but I am not systematic about it. • I "check in" with students, but I do not record my observations. • I occasionally use my observations as teaching points.	• I regularly analyze student strategy use. • I systematically document student reading behaviors when I "check in" with them. • I frequently use my observations as teaching points.	• I engage in thorough, ongoing analysis of student strategic reading. • I maintain a consistent and manageable record-keeping system. • I consistently use observations as "in-the-moment" teaching points and topics for future lessons.

Created by Susan Trask.

Practical Literacy Coaching: A Collection of Tools to Support Your Work by Jan Miller Burkins.
© 2009 International Reading Association. May be copied for classroom use.

Orientation to Tool 19:
ABCD Text-Rendering Protocol

In the opening of this chapter, I described three ideas that are central to developing and supporting professional learning communities in your school. I return to these here, as they are all connected to the use of protocols in professional learning. David Allen and Tina Blythe (2004) explain that "a protocol-guided conversation aims at enabling educators and interested others to learn more deeply about teaching and learning" (p. 11). Protocols are structures—or a series of interactive steps—that a group agrees to follow to involve everyone in systematic ways. They direct inquiry in particular directions, maintaining boundaries actualized by a facilitator, but they are open-ended enough to lead to discovery. Amy Sandvold and Maelou Baxter (2008) write,

> Most literacy coaches are teachers, and as teachers we constantly analyze our students' learning and our methods of teaching. Yet somehow, when the task shifts to teaching adults, we fail to apply what we learn from our "real" (i.e., younger) students. (p. 43)

When literacy coaches engage teachers in protocols, which are inherently learner focused and driven, the learning they experience is often profound. Cheryl Dozier (2006) comments, "Continuous inquiry leads to substantive rather than superficial changes" (p. 141).

As I maintained earlier, professional learning that elevates the capacity of a faculty to grow professionally is inherently self-extending. Toward this end, I have included a protocol that facilitates individual and group interaction with text. Sharon Smith, a member of the 2007 University of Georgia Literacy Coach Cohort, submitted the ABCD Text-Rendering Protocol.

ABCD TEXT-RENDERING PROTOCOL

Context: Analysis, criticism, and summary of a commonly read text

Time: 5 minutes for introduction, 10 minutes for writing, four rotations with each member of the group taking 2 minutes to speak, 10 minutes to debrief the protocol

Procedure

1. Divide participants into group sizes based on the amount of time you are planning for the protocol.
2. Give participants time to read the handout.
3. Assign a time keeper.
4. Distribute the protocol page for written responses.
5. Give everyone in the group 10 minutes to write a response to the ABCD prompts.
6. Prompt participants to begin rotations.
7. Debrief protocol by encouraging participants to talk about what they liked and disliked about it.

ABCD Text-Rendering Protocol Handout

A is for Alignment—With what points from the text do you agree?

B is for Bridging—What bridges can you construct between the text and your own personal teaching experiences?

C is for Conflict or Controversy—Were there any areas of the text that you questioned?

D is for Discussion—Discuss the connections you make among your experience, the text, and the collective knowledge of the group.

Rounds

First round—Each person has 2 minutes to share their responses to "A is for Alignment." The other group members listen but do not respond.

Second round—Each person has 2 minutes to share their responses to "B is for Bridging." The other group members listen but do not respond.

Third round—Each person has 2 minutes to share their responses to "C is for Conflict or Controversy." The other group members listen but do not respond.

Fourth round—Each person has 2 minutes to share their responses to "D is for Discussion." All members are encouraged to speak freely.

Created by Sharon Smith.

Practical Literacy Coaching: A Collection of Tools to Support Your Work by Jan Miller Burkins.
© 2009 International Reading Association. May be copied for classroom use.

Orientation to Tools 20–22: Instruments for Gathering Data on Your Effectiveness

One of the best ways to increase your effectiveness in supporting professional learning communities is to invite teachers to communicate the ways you can better meet their needs. Such an exercise not only gives you valuable information about the specific ways you can grow as a facilitator but also demonstrates your commitment to continuous reflection and self-improvement, a valuable model in a school.

The following three tools are for you to use to collect feedback from participants in professional learning you are facilitating. It is easy for a literacy coach who works consistently with a group of teachers to fall out of the habit of asking participants to evaluate the learning time. However, even coaches familiar with the teachers in their school need to consistently solicit feedback and to support teacher reflection on the ways to improve the work of a learning community.

Douglas Fisher and his colleagues at San Diego State University developed the first feedback tool that follows—Professional Learning Expectations Rubric. It is comprehensive in that it invites qualitative and quantitative responses for each area of feedback. The second instrument, Professional Development Workshop Scale, was developed by Michael Shaw from St. Thomas Aquinas College in Sparkill, New York, USA. It has a quantitative focus built around a workshop format. Susan Trask submitted the final evaluation tool, Professional Learning Reflection and Feedback Grid, which I value for its simplicity, its open-ended format, and its invitation to action.

PROFESSIONAL LEARNING
EXPECTATIONS RUBRIC

Professional learning session title _____

Put a check mark in the column indicating your opinions about the professional learning.
1 = Inadequate; 2 = Marginal; 3 = Adequate; 4 = Strong

Expectations	Comments	1	2	3	4
Content of professional development plan ✓ Design was effective ✓ Focus was clear and appropriate ✓ Addressed needs of participants					
Facilitation skills ✓ Engaged the participants ✓ Shared information confidently ✓ Communicated clearly					
Interpersonal skills ✓ Listened to concerns and questions ✓ Demonstrated care for the participants					
Knowledge base ✓ Is persuasive ✓ Inspired confidence because literacy coach has expertise					
Environment ✓ The work space was comfortable. ✓ We had the materials we needed to be productive.					

Other comments _____
_____
_____
_____

Suggestions for future professional learning _____
_____
_____
_____

Created by Douglas Fisher and colleagues at San Diego State University.

Practical Literacy Coaching: A Collection of Tools to Support Your Work by Jan Miller Burkins.
© 2009 International Reading Association. May be copied for classroom use.

PROFESSIONAL DEVELOPMENT
WORKSHOP SCALE

Title _____
Date _____

For each question, please circle the response that best indicates your feelings about the workshop.

SA = Strongly agree   A = Agree   N = Neutral   D = Disagree   SD = Strongly disagree

1. The literacy coach was enthusiastic and motivated me to want to learn.
   SA   A   N   D   SD

2. The literacy coach communicated effectively.
   SA   A   N   D   SD

3. The literacy coach communicated important information and strategies that I can use to enrich literacy learning with my class.
   SA   A   N   D   SD

4. The literacy coach effectively explained and demonstrated what was being taught.
   SA   A   N   D   SD

5. The literacy coach engaged me by providing opportunities for hands-on involvement.
   SA   A   N   D   SD

6. The literacy coach facilitated worthwhile discussion.
   SA   A   N   D   SD

7. The literacy coach used technology in ways that helped me learn.
   SA   A   N   D   SD

8. The literacy coach provided helpful resources.
   SA   A   N   D   SD

9. The professional development workshop was well organized.
   SA   A   N   D   SD

10. This was an excellent professional development workshop.
    SA   A   N   D   SD

Comments or suggestions to support learning (use back as needed):

Created by Michael Shaw.

Practical Literacy Coaching: A Collection of Tools to Support Your Work by Jan Miller Burkins.
© 2009 International Reading Association. May be copied for classroom use.

PROFESSIONAL LEARNING REFLECTION AND FEEDBACK GRID

As a result of this session,

I think	I wish
I hope	I will

I'd like more information about and support with _____

_____

_____

Name (optional)_____

_____

Created by Susan Trask.

Practical Literacy Coaching: A Collection of Tools to Support Your Work by Jan Miller Burkins.
© 2009 International Reading Association. May be copied for classroom use.

A Coaching Story:
Modeling in Professional Learning

I have been telling teachers for more than 15 years that any time they can use pair-share in their classrooms they increase the level of students' engagement and the learning of their classroom as a whole: If you are going to ask a question, ask it of the whole class rather than one student. How can you involve everyone in the work rather than asking one person to engage?

As I noted at the opening of this chapter, I have also made a commitment to teaching teachers in ways that I am asking them to teach students. I recently realized that I was not being true to this commitment when it came to pair-share.

My principal asked me to facilitate some whole-faculty professional learning—a format I loathe because it is so hard to differentiate for teacher needs—around levels of student engagement in lessons. It was late in the afternoon, and my time was limited. I worked hard to plan a learning session that would involve teachers in meaningful work. However, in debriefing I asked questions and looked for individuals to respond. This was particularly ineffective considering that I was working with more than 40 teachers in a cafeteria at 4:30 pm. Understandably, teachers were engaged in side conversations, and only a few participants were raising their hands to respond.

Suddenly, I realized that I was doing the exact opposite of what I have been asking them to do with students. I was in the middle of a professional learning session on student engagement, and the teachers were unengaged! So I regrouped and said, "I'm going to do this differently." I repeated the question and asked them to answer it with the person sitting next to them. Then I called on several pairs to share what they had discussed. The change in participation and engagement was dramatic, and teachers noticed it, too. I have seen more pair-share in classrooms since that professional learning session than I did after years of visiting classrooms and suggesting it. Not to mention that the switch in my practice made the professional learning session more engaging and valuable for the teachers.

LINK TO COACHING FOR BALANCE

For a global evaluation for teachers to use to give you feedback on your work as a coach, see the Literacy Coach Evaluation on page 203.

Coaching Connection:
The Rubik's Cube

Developing professional learning that is engaging and valuable for teachers is a constant challenge for literacy coaches. In fact, the professional learning within a building is usually made up of so many structures and contexts, each varying in its potential to support particular types of learning, that coaches may find themselves trying to solve puzzles. Michael McKenna and Sharon Walpole (2008) refer to this dilemma; they write, "Professional development systems that work are actually elegant solutions to problems in the real life of teachers" (p. 101).

Recently, as I was trying to mix and match the needs of the teachers in my school and the various contexts in which I can engage them in professional work, I became stymied by the myriad permutations and combinations. I finally wrote all of the needs on sticky notes in one color (questioning, running record analysis, text selection for guided reading, and so forth) and all the contexts on sticky notes of another color (grade-level meetings, professional learning days, study groups, faculty meetings, and so forth). Then I physically moved sticky notes in an effort to make some decisions. This was helpful first because the sticky nature of the adhesive notes is inherently forgiving—that is, I could change my mind about how I placed them. This meant that I could push my thinking beyond the walls I had encountered with pencil and paper. After I manipulated the notes enough, a solution became apparent. Second, once arranged in relationship to each other, the sticky notes became a graphic organizer that represented the way various aspects of my upcoming work were connected.

I heard a piece on National Public Radio called "Accomplishing Big Things in Small Pieces" (Ardalan, 2008), which reminded me of the experience I had using sticky notes to find resolution when I was overwhelmed and confused. It was part of the "I Believe" series and was an essay written and read by William Wisseman, an 18-year-old boy with a learning disability who was skilled in solving the Rubik's Cube. He observed, "I discovered that just before it's solved, a problem can look like a mess, and then suddenly you can find the solution. I believe that progress comes in unexpected leaps."

I agree with William; this has certainly been my experience as a literacy coach. I encourage you to push through the challenges that face you as you try to facilitate and scaffold the professional learning of the teachers with whom you work. A resolution may be closer than you think.

Resources for Developing and Supporting Learning Communities

Seven Spectacular Read-Alouds for Professional Learning

1. For a workshop on writing, making text-to-self connections, or responding to literature, read "Poetic Form: A Personal Encounter" by

Eavan Boland, which is part of the introductory material to *The Making of a Poem: A Norton Anthology of Poetic Forms* by Mark Strand and Eavan Boland (2000). In this piece Boland beautifully details the relationship between text and self. While she is writing about a poet's use of form, this essay makes explicit the ways that our experiences inform our exchanges with text. She writes of when her father first read her William Blake's "The Tyger." Then she talks of the experiences that were waiting in her head to greet this poem as she listened to it. She tells of getting lost in the lion house in a zoo and how this experience influences the way she responds to the poem, even suggesting that her experience in the lion house was somehow completed by the hearing of this poem. Boland writes,

> The lines of the poem do not quite enter a clear space. There is something waiting for them. As their music and emphasis enters the strange, foggy room through a human voice they are met by the memory of summer light and fear. And so even as the words of the poem happen, they are already arranging, in the most subtle and powerful way, experiences that have already happened. They are cutting across time and completed experience to show that, after all, it was incomplete (p. xxvii).

2. For a humorous introduction to any professional learning, read from *Teacher Man* by Frank McCourt (2005). While this book does have a rather depressing tone running through it, you can pull out some entertaining excerpts to share with teachers. My favorite is the portion in the introduction where McCourt details the fantasies he had of teaching before he became a teacher. He writes,

> Principals and other figures of authority passing in the hallways will hear sounds of excitement from your room. They'll peer through the door window in wonder at all the raised hands, the eagerness and excitement on the faces of these boys and girls.... You'll be nominated for awards: Teacher of the Year, Teacher of the Century. You'll be invited to Washington. Eisenhower will shake your hand. Newspapers will ask you, a mere teacher for your opinion on education. This will be big news. (p. 6)

The fantasy continues as McCourt imagines that he is courted by Hollywood producers and directors who want to make his life movie. He deliberates over who will play his mother, his father. Then he goes on to explain how he eventually "resisted the siren call of Hollywood" (p. 7) while he

> had become an idol and an icon in Hollywood, how they, the ravishing female stars, established and aspiring, regretted how they had gone astray, embracing the emptiness of their Hollywood lives when, if they gave it all up, they could rejoice daily in the integrity of teaching. (p. 7)

3. For any professional learning related to literacy in general and learning to read specifically, read from *Mama Makes Up Her Mind and Other Dangers of Southern Living* by Bailey White (1993). Bailey White was a first-grade teacher in Georgia and is now a writer. Her vignette "Maritime Disasters" is all about teaching first graders how to read using stories about the Titanic. She writes, "When children get the idea that written words can tell them something absolutely horrible, half the battle of teaching reading is won" (p. 170). The piece is both hilarious and moving, ending with White recognizing the victims of the Titanic tragedy.

> And some afternoons when the children are gone home, I sit all alone in my empty classroom surrounded by sketches of a wall-eyed Captain Smith and wonder if my use of the *Titanic* is not just as exploitative. Then I remind myself that in my whole career the *Titanic* and I will teach over a thousand children how to read—close to the number of people who lost their lives on that black night. (p. 172)

4. To illustrate the influence of teachers and our need to attend to children's emotional as well as academic needs, read Sandra Cisneros's (1991) essay "Eleven" from *Woman Hollering Creek and Other Stories*. This is the story of a little girl whose teacher is insensitive to her on her 11th birthday and how the humiliation of the day overshadows her celebration. Cisneros's writing is poetic and profound. It is worth reading her work aloud to a group simply for the sake of hearing the way she assembles words. Her prose is magic when spoken. She writes,

> What they don't understand about birthdays and what they never tell you is that when you're eleven, you're also ten, and nine, and eight, and seven, and six, and five, and four, and three, and two, and one.... Because the way you grow old is kind of like an onion or like the rings inside a tree trunk or like my little wooden dolls that fit one inside the other, each year inside the next one. That's how being eleven years old is. (pp. 6–7)

5. For a professional learning session on writing specifically, or on anything related to literacy in general, read from *Better Than Life* by Daniel Pennac (1994). The entire book is about a father's experience as his son is learning to read and write, and it is rich with text to read aloud to teachers. My favorite parts are when he is writing about reading aloud to his son and when he writes about his son learning to write *Mommy*. The latter is a piece with which I have to exercise great focus to get through without absolutely sobbing. Here is the excerpt from the moment after the child has succeeded in writing *Mommy!* and realized the connection between the word and his own mother.

> It wasn't *any* mother, it was *his* mother, a magical transformation, infinitely more eloquent than the most faithful photographic likeness, built from

nothing but little circles and sticks and bridges, that have now suddenly—and forever!—become more than scratches on paper. They have become her presence, her voice, the good way she smelled this morning, her lap, that infinity of details, that wholeness, so intimately absolute, and so absolutely foreign to what is written there, on the rails of the page, within the four walls of the classroom. (p. 47)

6. For any group of teachers, particularly first-grade teachers, "All Aboard" from *Loser* by Jerry Spinelli (2002) puts a new spin on the idea of a school career. It takes place in Miss Meeks's first-grade classroom on the first day of her last year of teaching. The excerpt that follows comes immediately after she has calculated how many days the new first graders will be in school by the time they graduate.

> Two thousand one hundred and sixty. The days of your journey. That is how long your adventure will last. Every one of those days will be an opportunity to learn something new. Just *imagine* how much you can learn in two thousand one hundred and sixty days!" She pauses to let them imagine. (p. 16)

Miss Meeks ends her opening day speech as follows:

> She reaches into her desk drawer and pulls out the old, navy blue train conductor's cap. For the thirty-first and last time she puts it on. She pumps her hand twice. "Toot! Toot! All aboard the Learning Train! First stop, Writing My Own Name! Who's coming aboard?" Twenty six hands shoot into the air. And Zinkoff, jumping to his feet so fast that he knocks his desk over with a nerve-slapping racket, thrusts up his hands and bellows to the ceiling: "YAHOO!" (p.17)

7. One of the strongest pieces I have read aloud to groups in professional learning has been Chapter 15 of *Elijah of Buxton* by Christopher Paul Curtis (2007). It is ideal for a professional learning session dealing with writers' workshop in general or revision specifically. The chapter, entitled "Keeping Mr. John Holton Alive," is so powerful that the participants in your session will go straight to the book store from your workshop so that they can purchase their own copy. Be warned, however, that you must practice reading this one a few hundred times to achieve a level of numbness before reading it aloud in front of a group. Otherwise, you will dissolve into a heap in the middle of the reading. This chapter offers a dramatic illustration of the power of words and the role of revision in the writing process. Elijah revises the words that are to be carved above the doorway of a woman who, now living in Canada as a free woman, wants to remember her husband who died trying to escape to be with her. I read the whole chapter aloud to groups. For the sake of brevity, I share the "before" and "after" of the writing to go above the door. Mrs. Holton writes,

These words is done so no one won't never forget the loving memory of my husband John Holton what got whip to death and killed on May the seven 1859 just 'cause he want to see what his family look like if they free. He be resting calm knowing his family done got through. The body won't never endure but something inside all of us be so strong it always be flying. (p.215)

The chapter describes Elijah's process of wrestling with the words, getting help from his teacher, and how Mrs. Holton responds when Elijah reads them to her. He reads, "For the love of my husband, John Holton, who passed on May 7th, 1859, but still lives. The body is not made to endure. There's something inside so strong it flies forever" (p. 221).

Four Books to Support Coaches in Facilitating Professional Learning

1. *The Power of Protocols: An Educator's Guide to Better Practice* (2nd ed.) by Joseph P. McDonald, Nancy Mohr, Alan Dischter, and Elizabeth C. McDonald offers a rationale for using protocols to support inquiry and dialogue in professional learning. It also includes a collection of protocols.

2. *Looking Together at Student Work* (2nd ed.) by Tina Blythe, David Allen, and Barbara Schieffelin Powell (2008) looks closely at the "why" and the "how" of examining student work. It offers specific support for the facilitator of a learning community and includes a set of tools.

3. *Tools for Leaders* by Marjorie Larner (2007) is rooted in the work of educators in the field and is supported by the National School Reform Faculty. The book is packed with the tools that are the cornerstone of Critical Friends Groups throughout the United States.

4. *Writing for a Change: Boosting Literacy and Learning Through Social Action* is put together by the National Writing Project (2006). It includes a collection of excellent protocols that can be used with students. However, they can be adapted to support adult professional learning communities.

Taking Chapter 4 Personally: How Are You Developing and Supporting Learning Communities in *Your* School?

Questions for Further Reflection

• What are the professional learning priorities for the teachers in your school? How do you know? How will you help them meet their needs?

- Describe the learning community in your school relative to its learning history? How has the learning community in your school grown and changed? What will you do to help it develop further?

- How do you assess yourself as a facilitator of professional learning? How effective is your method of assessment? How do you know?

Possible Action Steps

- Write the professional learning topics that are pressing for your faculty on individual sticky notes of one color. Write the professional learning contexts in which you can work with them on individual sticky notes of another color. Physically move the sticky notes to strategically examine your priorities and make decisions.

- Gather agendas from several professional learning sessions that you have recently facilitated. Examine them through the lens of inquiry? How did you provide the participants in your session opportunities to interact with one another and with the information in ways that supported them as they negotiated their own understandings?

CHAPTER 5

Coaching Individual Teachers

"When we look into our selves and discover what is radiant and dull, ugly and beautiful, clear and confusing, harsh and gentle, it isn't just ourselves we're discovering; we're unfolding the mysteries of the universe."
Irwin Kula

Opening Thoughts: Records on the Run

The magic of running records rests in two parallel elements. First, running records are comprehensive by design. They are a relatively complete reflection of a text, literally word by word, from starting point to finishing point. Even when running records only capture a portion of a reading, they are an attempt at inclusively representing a child's negotiations with that particular collection of connected graphemes from the first word to the last, including the hiccup in the middle.

Second, for the most part, running records are objective. They are quite simply a straightforward record of how a student integrates sources of information while reading a particular passage. What a child says in response to the text is transcribed, and much of the time, this is just a matter of record that requires little discussion or debate. Even if nuances are disputed or the "running" nature of classroom assessment makes the record understandably less than comprehensive, the heart of a child's reading process is usually represented consistently through the documentation of patterns or repeated behaviors.

The transcriptions of teacher talk during classroom lessons mirror running records and can bring a similar element of magic to the supportive conversations we have with teachers who are reflecting on their practice. Such straightforward records of the language of instruction provide objective fodder for discussions. Several of the tools that I share in this section are designed to approximate running-record–type watching and recording in classrooms, thus providing teachers with their own scripts to buttress their reflection.

You will find no checklists in this section, as I think that visiting classrooms with checklists when teachers had no role in their development implies supervision and carries with it an overt display of power. Rather, the tools that I include here for documenting what you see and hear in classrooms are designed to help you do two things. First, they all boast some element of scripting inherent in their design. As Dozier (2006) writes, "The transcription of the lesson provides multiple points of view for the conversation and grounds it in the language of the lesson" (p. 83). Second, they are designed around a strengths perspective; that is, they work from the assumptions of goodwill that I presented at the beginning of this book.

Coaching Connection: Thinking Outside the Mailbox

In visiting classrooms to watch instruction, a coach can offer a fresh pair of eyes. Sometimes you can see something that a classroom teacher has overlooked in the fog of familiarity. My friend recently brought home to me the value of enlisting an outside perspective.

My family lives downtown, and we have to park our car on the street. Unfortunately, the spot on the street in front of our house, the one connected by sidewalk to our front door, the one most convenient for delivering children and unloading groceries, is also right in front of our mailbox. In the last year, I have become familiar with the laws regarding mail delivery and the proximity of parked vehicles relative to the mailbox. However, the inconvenience of our alternate parking place prompts us to unload people and things and then move the car. Despite our vigilance, we sometimes forget to move the car and then we risk the wrath of our postperson.

We have received a series of unkind, handwritten notes from our mailperson, warning us of our risk of being cut off from all mail. We have had tense follow-up communications with our local postmaster general, who encouraged us to keep documentation of our notes from our mailperson and to send this documentation to her. I awake at 2:00 a.m. some Saturday mornings in a cold sweat wondering, Did we move the car? The amount of stress associated with getting our mail has been startling. I literally think of some aspect of this issue almost every day.

About a week ago I was talking with a couple of friends, and I was telling them about the situation. I elaborated on our struggle and the time-consuming efforts we had invested in simply getting our mail. I talked of meetings with the postmaster, time at a copier documenting notes left by the mailman, even loss of sleep.

My friend, who also happens to be a literacy coach, looked puzzled. He paused for just a second and said, "Well, why don't you just move the mailbox to the other side of the street?" I was floored by the simplicity of this solution. How had we missed such an obvious option? Our thinking had been trapped within the proverbial box, and I needed a coach to recast our situation.

When we are entangled in a problem, we are often the least capable of identifying simple solutions. On a classroom level, the literacy coach is that outside set of eyes, that brain that is not emotionally intertwined in the complexities of a situation, that person who can open the box that is limiting a teacher's thinking. Whatever the context, the outside perspective of a coach can offer teachers fresh alternatives.

Related Research:
Feedback and Situated Identities

While the research on literacy coaching has been expanding rapidly, until recently few researchers had examined the complexities of the various interactions between coaches and teachers. In "Situated Identities: Power and Positioning in the Work of a Literacy Coach," Kristin Rainville and Stephanie Jones (2008) write about these dynamic interactions and draw on three case studies conducted by Rainville (2007).

They examine the work of Kate, a practicing literacy coach, and analyze three transcripts of Kate's conversations with three different teachers in three very different contexts. Rainville and Johnson draw from the transcript data three practical literacy lessons for literacy coaches. First, power struggles were less of a barrier to productive work when the coach and the teacher had established an informal relationship. Second, when the coach self-positions as a colearner or coparticipant, teachers are more likely to feel a sense of agency regarding their professional development and more likely to experiment with concepts that could have an impact on their instructional practices. Finally, as supported by the previously mentioned research of Johnson-Lambert (2008), when the teacher and coach perspectives on the role of the coach are incongruent, misunderstandings and miscommunications may lead to "a counterproductive standoff" (p. 447). It is critical that coaches communicate effectively, but there is room for error if you are reflective and getting better at your interactions with teachers. One way to set yourself up for success is to consider upfront your situated identity relative to the teacher and communicate clearly with teachers by engaging in a preobservation conference. An instrument for supporting these initiating discussions opens the collection of tools in this chapter.

Tools for Coaching Individual Teachers

Orientation to Tool 23:
Preobservation Conference Record

I designed this tool primarily to guide my coaching cycles with teachers by setting in place a "formal" preobservation phase. This tool requires me to be thoughtful around my preobservation work in ways that more casual preliminary conferences can't. It also formalizes for teachers my interest in remaining faithful to their priorities for my visit. The observation cycle generally includes conferring with teachers before and after visiting a classroom to watch a lesson, but when I use this tool to support these conversations I find that the teacher and I have fewer misunderstandings and I am more focused in my observations. Thus, the embedded opportunity for teachers to direct the focus of the literacy coach becomes a demonstration of trust and a manifestation of the assumptions of goodwill that I try to let shape my coaching. By following the teacher's lead, a literacy coach acknowledges the teacher's power in the classroom and proffers a tangible demonstration that the coach is visiting in a supportive role.

In addition, the preobservation conference gives the coach an opportunity to gain insight into a teacher's professional reflection. This insight is fodder for building on teacher strengths and for thoughtfully responding to teachers in ways that consider their professional learning stance. Furthermore, an advantage of following the teacher's lead in the classroom visitation is that the starting point for the postobservation conference is already established, as the coach responds to what happened in the classroom relative to the need the teacher identified. This data collection is usually perceived by the teacher as supportive work because the coach is acting at his or her request.

> **LINK TO COACHING FOR BALANCE**
>
> The companion to the pre- and postobservation tools included here is the Classroom Visitation Feedback Form on page 127 in Chapter 7. A blank copy is available in the Appendix to *Coaching for Balance*. See also the Sample Classroom Visitation Record on page 136. This record is for documenting all your classroom visits on one page.

PREOBSERVATION CONFERENCE RECORD

Coach _____ Teacher_____ Date_____

Lesson	Guided reading		Writer's workshop		Working with words	
	Shared reading		Independent reading		Read-aloud	
	Other					

Lesson description

What the coach said/asked	What the teacher said/asked

Coaching focus

PREOBSERVATION CONFERENCE RECORD
SAMPLE

Coach ___Burkins___ Teacher ___Smith___ Date ___12-5-05___

Lesson	Guided reading		Writer's workshop	X	Working with words	
	Shared reading		Independent reading		Read-aloud	
	Other					

Lesson description
Teacher is going to use a list of prewritten sentences in the minilesson to get students to decide where and what type of punctuation is needed.

What the coach said/asked	What the teacher said/asked
What do you anticipate as the challenges your students will face with this lesson? What are their strengths?	The strength is that they love to write and illustrate their writing. The challenge is that their vocabularies are so limited. More specifically, we are doing this lesson because they just don't use ending punctuation in their writing.
So, is it safe to say that the goal for the lesson is for them to begin to use ending punctuation independently?	Yes.
How will you scaffold their move to independence?	Well, I hope the minilesson helps. Also, I'm going to circulate and help them look at their writing individually.
Is there anything in particular you want me to watch for?	I'm interested in what they are doing independent of me. I have a hard time seeing what they are doing when I am working with other students.

Coaching focus
What are students doing during independent writing time when the teacher is working with individual students?

Orientation to Tool 24: Workshop Venn Diagram

This is another one of my favorite tools in this book because it clearly illustrates how the focus of a lesson is an undercurrent through every part of a workshop, whether reading workshop or writing workshop. For example, when I began using writers' workshop to teach writing, it was not uncommon for me to teach a minilesson on one topic—writing interesting leads, for example—and then spend the rest of the time conferring with writers on other matters. This means that the sharing portion of the workshop was usually disconnected from the minilesson because I was not intentional about supporting and seeking out writers who were exploring the topic of the minilesson. Understanding the circular connection between the minilesson and the sharing, by way of the workshop session and conferences, represented a real milestone in my thinking about reading and writing workshops. In the early literature on writers' workshop, such overt teaching was considered too explicit and not organic enough, so my professional thinking on this matter has evolved. Now I see a workshop lesson format as a completely unified entity with all parts working toward a focused priority.

In the following graphic organizer, the overlap of the circles within the Venn diagram serves as a place to make notes about the concentrated focus of the lesson and the way the parts of the workshop are connected. For example, at the end of the minilesson, how did the teacher charge the students with applying their new learning? As students transitioned from the writing time to sharing, did the teacher identify some students for sharing based on their application of the principle from the minilesson? Finally, how did the teacher utilize the sharing time to further reinforce the concept he or she introduced in the minilesson?

By writing the focus of the lesson in the center of the diagram and using other parts to document connections between and across the work within the components of the workshop, the literacy coach can capture the cyclical nature of a workshop and help teachers examine how these various components support one another. This form reaches beyond the sample writing workshop lesson and is relevant for other workshop formats as well, such as readers' workshop, spelling workshop, even math or science workshops.

This document has been a powerful tool in my work with teachers as it has opened up their understandings of how the various components of a workshop are connected. Teachers have expressed enthusiasm and experienced "ahas" as they have seen the ways that their lessons map onto this form. As is often the case with a strong tool, this document has had a powerful impact on classroom instruction in my school.

WORKSHOP VENN DIAGRAM

Teacher _____ Visitor _____ Date _____

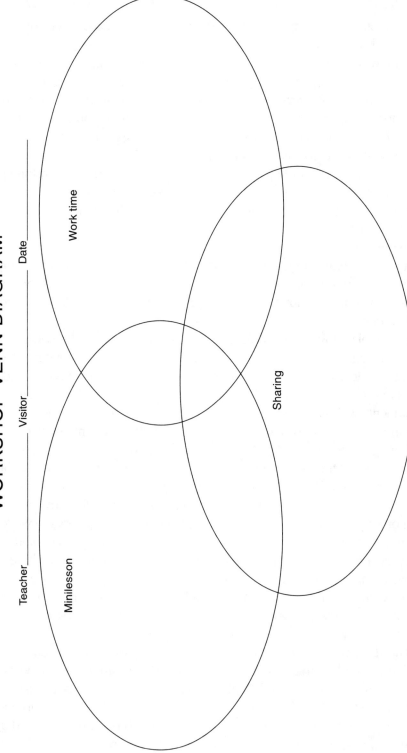

Minilesson

Work time

Sharing

WORKSHOP VENN DIAGRAM SAMPLE

Teacher_____ Visitor_____ Date_____

Minilesson 8:15

Teacher used *The Very Hungry Caterpillar* to illustrate how the author's pictures and words matched. She pulled out guided reading books from student browsing boxes and found more examples. Students had a couple of minutes to look at their guided reading books and share with a partner places where the pictures and the print matched.

Work time 9:00

Teacher circulated and helped some students examine their work to see if their pictures and words matched. Helped students develop a plan for correcting problems. Teacher also helped students with their writing priorities.

Teacher prompted students to make sure that their pictures and words matched in their writing.

Pictures and words match

Teacher pre-selected students to share how their pictures and words match.

Teacher reinforced minilesson focus during sharing.

Sharing 9:30

Six students shared. Students sat in a circle on the rug. Teacher facilitated. Children asked questions of each other and gave compliments.

Orientation to Tool 25:
Small-Group Conversation Log

This simple and elegant tool, contributed by Darcie St. Onge from the 2007 University of Georgia Literacy Coach Cohort, presents an organized approach to scripting the conversations of a lesson. There is space to document what a teacher says to students and how students respond to the teacher. It is a sort of "running record" of teacher and student exchange that lets the coach and teacher go back and re-create the lesson. The Small-Group Conversation Log even allows for overlap in conversations. The beauty of this form is that there is no subjectivism in it; it is simply a written record of what took place in the lesson.

The Small-Group Conversation Log also documents patterns in response that a teacher might be making unwittingly. It is apparent, after completing this form, if the teacher unconsciously favors or overlooks particular children. Capturing objective data like this is powerful, because it can support teachers as they explore their biases. The discoveries they make about their patterns of language and behavior are more likely to be meaningful and prompt change than those that a literacy coach points out. Often times, teachers will see even more in a script than we notice ourselves, as they are intrinsically motivated by their own drive to improve. You can vary your use of this tool by using it to simply document which students the teacher is calling on. The boxes under each child's name could be filled with tally marks representing the number of times each one responded to the teacher.

Another thing I appreciate about this and the other tools that support coaches as they gather the verbatim (as much as is possible) language of the classroom is that there is absolute transparency in the documentation. That is, you do not collect data on a form that is for you to study and file, but rather you gather data to the benefit of the teacher. Everything captured on a record such as this is there to be shared with the teacher.

SMALL-GROUP CONVERSATION LOG

Teacher_____ Date_____ Text_____

What the teacher said	What the students said				
Teacher					

Created by Darcie St. Onge.

Practical Literacy Coaching: A Collection of Tools to Support Your Work by Jan Miller Burkins. © 2009 International Reading Association. May be copied for classroom use.

TOOL
25

SMALL-GROUP CONVERSATION LOG SAMPLE

Teacher ___Smith___   Date _9-4-07_ Text _Amelia Bedelia_

What the teacher said	What the students said					
Teacher	Sam	Lucy	Damian	Tondrea	Patrick	Lucia
Do any of you remember what I told you we were going to do today?	Comprehension quiz	Comprehension quiz		Comprehension quiz	Comprehension quiz	
And you know why I'm so excited—because I know you're all going to do great! Before we get started, I have a few questions. Since we're almost done with the book, I'm wondering what your favorite part is.	When Amelia Bedelia cuts up the dress.			She cut the dress.		
Whose dress did she cut up, and why was it so funny?	She wasn't supposed to cut it.		No. That was not what she was supposed to do.			_shaking head_
What was she supposed to do?	She was supposed to clean the stains...she cut them up.			Wash it.		
How would you feel if you came home and your mom had cut up your favorite jeans?	Ewww!	No way!	_shaking head_	Mad!	That's bad!	
So instead of getting the stains out in the laundry she got them out by cutting up the dress. What was your favorite part?		When she threw the roses in the air.		Me too!		

(continued)

SMALL-GROUP CONVERSATION LOG SAMPLE *(continued)*

Teacher _Smith_   Date _9-4-07_   Text _Amelia Bedelia_

What the teacher said	What the students said					
Teacher	Sam	Lucy	Damian	Tondrea	Patrick	Lucia
Don't forget I need to hear the end of your words. What was she suppose to do with the roses? Look on page 52. Do you remember the word that Ms. Rogers used?		Scatter.			Scatter.	
		What does scatter mean?				
Look at the picture.		Oh, like put them all over.		Spread them out.		
Scatter all over the place, lay them all over, that's right. Let's go ahead and start reading.	reading quietly	reading quietly	reading to teacher	reading quietly	reading quietly	looking around room
			I need help.			
It's a contraction. Do you know what that contraction is?		They're...they are.				
Teacher moves to second student.	reading quietly	reading to teacher	reading quietly	reading quietly	reading quietly	looking around room
Slow down and make sure you say the endings.		student reading				

123

A Coaching Story: Learning to Script Lessons

While I usually take a form such as those included in the previous pages when I visit classrooms, I also take a legal pad that I use for scripting what a teacher says during the lesson. I use the term *scripting* loosely, as my final records are not comprehensive records of the lesson. My scripting tends to focus around the area of concern for the teacher or around patterns that I have noticed in the classroom previously. I will, necessarily, leave out other elements.

When I was first learning to script lessons, I really struggled with what to document and what to omit. I would work to record the lesson verbatim and get confused and behind. I do not process information very quickly, so these efforts were quite frustrating for me. However, while I am a slow processor, I am strong in analysis. I decided to work through a scripting exercise and try to think about my thinking. What I found was that, like many tasks we undertake, scripting a lesson involves two processes, so one must be automated to free up attention for the other.

To script a lesson, a coach must invest cognitive energy in sorting through the language exchanges and prioritizing them in an effort to make quick decisions about what to write down. I practiced this thinking part of the work; that is, I practiced scripting and focused on filtering through all the dialogue to concentrate on the language most relevant at the moment.

To simplify the documenting work, I use a bit of shorthand. I use ellipses when I don't think that the whole sentence needs to be captured. (e.g., "After you finish reading, I want you to go get your reading log from..."). Much of what I write down has at least a little paraphrasing, so when I review it with teachers I make sure they understand that it is an approximation, albeit a close approximation. If I am confident that I have captured a sentence exactly, then I put it in quotes. To indicate a change in speaker, I either indent (see example that follows) or write everything flush left and put in the left-hand margin either *T* for teacher or *S* for the student. Here is a sample:

"You got stuck, but you figured it out. What did you do?"

"I looked at the picture, and it was a picture of a dog. So I thought the word was *dog*."

"How did you check it?"

"I looked at the word and saw that it started with *d* so I thought it must be *dog*?"

"So you made sure what you were saying matched the words and the picture?"

"Yes."

Finally, since there may be whole portions of the lesson that are not relevant for scripting, I denote a passage of time, a transition, or an omission in the script with a horizontal line across my page.

> "Let's all move to a circle on the rug so that you can share your writing."
>
> "I asked Carrie to share because she really worked on revising her piece by putting in more interesting words."
>
> "Carrie, are you ready? I know you practiced reading your story."
>
> "Yes."
>
> "Now, while Carrie is reading, I want you to notice interesting or unusual words that she used in her story. Go ahead, Carrie."
>
> "Once upon a time..."
>
> _____
>
> "Thank you, Carrie. So what special words did you notice in Carrie's story?"

Scripting is an invaluable tool for working with teachers individually. The objective nature of scripting plays a critical role in establishing trust, as teachers understand that your notes are not judgmental. Most importantly, having these "running records" of classroom decision making and negotiations enables coaches and teachers to reflect in ways that are more meaningful than conversations that are in the abstract or drawn from tenuous memory. Such tools scaffold coaches and teachers reliably as they navigate the bumpy terrain of classroom change.

Coaching Connection: Just What I Needed

As literacy coaches, we sometimes find ourselves coaching in areas where our limited expertise only allows for approximations. In recognition of our limitations and in an effort to circumvent failure, most of us have avoided the mantle of "expert," so when we have to stretch ourselves to support teachers our risk is limited. Nonetheless, we sometimes feel that we need to know everything about an area of literacy or instruction to feel legitimate as a coach. However, an alternative coaching context recently demonstrated to me that this is not the case.

One of my twin sons is passionate about basketball and is currently preparing for basketball tryouts. Sometimes I take him to the YMCA, where he can practice dribbling and shooting. Occasionally, he will talk me into getting onto the basketball court with him.

I am painfully unathletic; I was the classic "last one picked" for every competitive physical education (PE) event. However, somewhere in the recesses (no pun intended) of my mind, I was able to pull up something a PE teacher taught us about how to hold the ball when trying to make a free throw. As it turns out, this was just the information that Duncan needed. He applied my advice and immediately improved his free throw. He was as surprised as I was that I had some basketball insight that improved his game.

In the earliest days of a literacy coaching role, a coach is usually trying to establish credibility with teachers. The coach is likely to want teachers to see him or her as a resource. However, it is possible to be a valuable resource without being an expert; if you carefully inventory the needs of teachers, you can often seek out a piece of information that really helps them become more successful. This nugget of truth may be just what the teacher with whom you are working may need, and one relevant and helpful piece of information is enough to make a difference in the classroom and establish your "expertise."

Resources for Coaching Individual Teachers

1. Marilyn Duncan's (2006) book *Literacy Coaching: Developing Effective Teachers through Instructional Dialogue* offers insights into the conversations Duncan has with teachers. The book is filled with her metacognition around coaching exchanges. It also has a DVD that shows a postobservation conference with a teacher. This clip is valuable fodder for discussing the language of coaching.

2. *The Literacy Coach's Companion* by Maryann Mraz, Bob Algozzine, and Brian Kissel (2009) is full of practical ideas and tools for working with teachers in a variety of contexts, including working with individuals.

Taking Chapter 5 Personally: How Will *You* Work With Individual Teachers?

Questions for Reflection

- How are you recording the work you see in classrooms? How do you manage objectivity?

- How are the tools you use to document instruction useful for supporting change?

- What evidence do you have that your classroom visits are affecting instruction?

Possible Action Steps

- Gather the instruments you use to document what you see and hear in classrooms. Analyze these tools through the lens of power. How do they respect teachers as the decision makers in their classrooms? If they don't, how can you modify them?

- Review your notes related to working with individual teachers. What patterns emerge? Now take a look at historic documentation of your work with a particular teacher. What connections can you make between these two sources of data? What gaps do you see?

CHAPTER 6

Documenting Your Work, Managing Your Time

"Time is that quality of nature which keeps events from happening all at once. Lately it doesn't seem to be working."
Anonymous

Opening Thoughts: Matters of Time

Ask teachers what they need and, without fail, they will respond, "Time." Literacy coaches are similarly overextended. When you consider the various tasks and responsibilities on the shoulders of coaches, the burden of "documentation" simply adds another layer to our efforts. Documenting our work is a paradoxical test: We run the risk of spending an inordinate amount of time recording our work and, consequently, of having less time to make an impact on classroom instruction.

Most books on literacy coaching counsel coaches to document their interactions with teachers. One form I recently examined was accompanied by directions that said something like, "Whenever you meet with a teacher to talk about an instructional issue or a student's progress, document your conversation in detail on this form." This charge betrays an obvious disconnect between the realities of literacy coaching and the theoretical role that documentation plays in the increasing accountability of coaches.

This chapter includes a collection of tools to help you document various aspects of your work. The tools were not developed to comprehensively detail every facet of your work with teachers. They are simply a resource for you to weigh the most important elements of your interactions with teachers. You will have to consider each of these through the lens of your literacy coaching context and resolve your own tensions between the work itself and the recording of it. This is one of the many precarious balancing acts of literacy coaching.

Coaching Connection: Drumming Class

My 5-year-old son is taking a drumming class. There are eight 3- to 5-year-old boys in the class, which is taught by Dr. Arvin Scott, a drumming professor at the University of Georgia. Dr. Scott is a genius at managing the energy of the group. He is conscious of each individual child and the child's contribution to the rhythm of the whole. His leadership of the class is always energetic and directed in response to the cues he receives from the class.

As the literacy coach, you have to consider how you manage your time. However, equally important, you have to consider the ways in which your time management influences the time of the teachers in your building. How do you respond to their cues? How do the pace and the rhythm that you influence in your school shape the work of teachers? As you plan for professional learning or work collaboratively with teachers, what does your utilization of time say about your commitments to reflection, urgency, or excellence? I encourage you to be thoughtful about your use of time both because it has an impact on your productivity and because you are setting a rhythm that can ring through your school and influence teachers.

Related Research: Energy and Time

As I suggested in the opening thoughts for this chapter, time is the elusive element in the lives of most educators. However, there is research that suggests that time is less the barrier to getting more work completed than our energy levels. Jim Loehr and Tony Schwartz (2003), authors of *The Power of Full Engagement: Managing Energy, Not Time, Is the Key to High Performance and Personal Renewal,* initially worked with world-class athletes. Their revolutionary research demonstrated that when athletes spent less time training and more time renewing, they actually improved in skill and efficiency. From athletes, their work expanded and today they are supporting teachers, lawyers, entrepreneurs, and others in managing their energy.

They suggest, "It is not the intensity of energy expenditure that produces burnout, impaired performance and physical breakdown, but rather the duration of expenditure without recovery" (p. 41). The field of education is not one that is widely known for its attention to the need for renewal. Nationally, about 50% of teachers leave their jobs within the first five years of teaching (Hernandez, 2007). Given the high turnover rate among new teachers and the burnout palpable in many schools, one might conclude that education actually works against taking care of educators' needs to renew themselves.

It is incumbent upon you, as a literacy coach, to take care of yourself, to balance the many competing demands of literacy coaching, and to

LINK TO COACHING FOR BALANCE

To read more about how taking care of yourself can actually improve your effectiveness at work, see Chapter 3.

manage your personal and professional resources in ways that increase your longevity in the field. While we race through our days with exclamations of "I need more time!" the reality may be that we simply need more energy to be more effective with the time we have. Loehr and Schwartz write, "Energy, not time, is the fundamental currency of high performance" (p. 4). Perhaps we would accomplish more in our work if we took care to renew ourselves professionally and personally.

Tools for Documenting Your Work and Managing Your Time

Orientation to Tool 26: Starting the School Year Checklist

Part of the effort of managing our work rests in simplifying recurring tasks rather than continually reinventing them. I have found that one way to accomplish this is to develop checklists that help me manage various elements of my work.

For example, it occurred to me at the beginning of this school year that there are certain tasks I do each fall to organize myself for the work of the upcoming year. In fact, my beginning-of-the-year to-do lists were surprisingly similar from year to year. I began to wonder why I was re-creating a "new" one each fall. I have other lists that support me as I plan professional learning events or navigate certain types of assessment data.

I include this Starting the School Year Checklist in this resource book as an example of how a checklist can increase your efficiency *and* document your work. I also hope that this particular example will prove useful for you, as it is pretty general and holds at least some applicability for most literacy coaches. Over the last few years this list has become refined, and I share it with you here in the hopes that it will help you as you organize your work. Where applicable, the tasks are cross-referenced with tool numbers that correspond to the forms in this book.

❑ Set up computer filing system.

❑ Obtain a complete list of the faculty and make teacher checklist document (see Tool 27). Make copies of the teacher checklist so that you have them when you need them.

❑ Obtain classroom rosters. Request updated copies of these periodically.

❑ Introduce yourself to new faculty.

❑ If you do not have a job description, research and write one (see Tool 3).

❑ If you do have a job description, print out a copy to determine how you will communicate it with the faculty.

❑ Review the instrument with which you will be evaluated.

❑ Set up weekly meetings with your administrator.

❑ Set your professional goals for the year.

❑ Develop a system for logging conference and observation notes.

❑ Obtain relevant assessment data from the previous year(s).

❑ Visit every classroom for 10–20 minutes without a clipboard in the first week of school.

❑ Write professional learning plans so that teachers will receive professional learning credit for time spent in site-based professional learning.

❑ Set up your calendar. Transfer in your district dates for professional learning days, end of terms, and so forth.

❑ Prepare introduction of yourself and how you can support teachers, and present this at an initial faculty meeting (see Tool 6).

❑ Develop system for teachers to request support (see Tool 7).

❑ Develop professional learning plan for yourself. Contact local coaches who may support you.

Orientation to Tool 27: Teacher Checklist

I assemble this tool at the beginning of each school year, and it is a tremendous timesaver for me. Prior to using this simple form, I created sticky notes or lists on my calendar that I later had to cross-reference or compile.

Now, I use a list such as this constantly to keep track of anything that requires me to communicate with each teacher. I fill in the headings on each column with a pen, based on the need of the moment. For example, at a given time, the chart might read "guided reading levels," "book requests," "professional learning." Using the chart, I can check off the teachers from whom I have received a list of the guided reading levels of their students, a list of books they need, and their completed professional learning surveys. Any time I have to distribute or collect or communicate something to teachers individually, I use this chart to keep track of my work.

This is probably the tool I use the most of all of those that I have shared with you. I obtain the faculty list promptly at the beginning of the school year and complete an electronic copy of this form. I print out a copy and make a stack of hard copies that I keep accessible. At any given time I have a couple of these working forms on my desk on which I am collecting an array of information.

Again, this is a tool that serves double-duty. It is both a record-keeping form to log your communications with teachers. However, it also houses data that, very simply, documents the nature of your work.

TEACHER CHECKLIST

	Grade	Work samples for professional learning	Lists of guided reading groups	Check if author study materials are in each classroom	Suggestions for guided reading books to order for bookroom
Bonnie	P	✓	✓		
Jennifer	P		✓		
Janice	K		✓	✓	✓
Miriam	K	✓			
Laura	K	✓	✓		✓
Melanie	1	✓	✓		
Carol	1	✓	✓	✓	✓
Fran	1	✓		✓	
Tanya	2		✓		
Raymond	2		✓		✓
Betsy	2	✓			
Candy	3		✓	✓	✓

Orientation to Tool 28: Study Group Conversation Log

Study groups are increasingly common in schools as teachers pursue investigations in areas of interest. The role of the literacy coach in these contexts is generally to help gather resources, organize a schedule, or facilitate the work of a group.

For purposes of record keeping, I like the conversation log by Leslie Barrett-Jones of the 2007 University of Georgia Literacy Coach Cohort because it offers a longitudinal view of the group's work. Any time a tool for data collection or documentation can capture a historical perspective so that the teachers and the coach can see patterns over time, it increases its value because it serves as both a learning tool as well as a form for accountability.

With this form, a study group can explore their learning over time. Are there recurring themes? Are there patterns of understanding or confusion? Are there indications of where this group should next take their investigations? Peter Johnston (2004) refers to this as our "learning histories" (p. 14)—or the changes in our work that we can observe and describe. A tool such as this conversation log offers a systematic record of a group's learning history.

Of course, as I mentioned previously, there are increasing accountability measures in schools, and this form meets that obligation without requiring a heavy time investment. It illustrates the basic elements of the work without extensive documentation.

STUDY GROUP CONVERSATION LOG

Title of book being studied _____

Author(s) _____

Session # _____ Date of this meeting _____ Chapter or pages read _____ Date of next meeting _____			
Group members present	Concepts discussed	Additional comments	Before next meeting...
Session # _____ Date of this meeting _____ Chapter or pages read _____ Date of next meeting _____			

Created by Leslie Barrett-Jones.

Practical Literacy Coaching: A Collection of Tools to Support Your Work by Jan Miller Burkins.
© 2009 International Reading Association. May be copied for classroom use.

STUDY GROUP CONVERSATION LOG SAMPLE

Title of book being studied _A Teacher's Guide to Standardized Reading Tests:_
Knowledge Is Power

Author(s) _Calkins, Montgomery, Falk, & Santman_

Session # _1_		Date of this meeting _3-16-07_	
Chapter or pages read _1_		Date of next meeting _3-30-07_	
Group members present	Concepts discussed	Additional comments	Before next meeting...
1. Linda Johnson 2. Shannon Smart 3. Millie Kennon 4. Louise Anderson 5. Anna Turner 6. Dorothy Peters	1. We really identified with the authors and their frustration. 2. Shared struggles with balancing test pressure with "real" teaching 3. Did the authors "sell out"? Why or why not.	We found the book easy to read and encouraging.	Read chapter 2
Session # _2_		Date of this meeting _3-30-07_	
Chapter or pages read _2_		Date of next meeting _1-13-07_	
1. Linda Johnson 2. Shannon Smart 3. Louise Anderson 4. Anna Turner 5. Dorothy Peters	1. Why do we believe standardized tests more than we believe other evidence of student progress? 2. What is the construct validity of our state's test? 3. Described students we have taught who have been like "Malik"	How would we go about finding out the construct validity of our state test? Does anyone really know how it was developed?	Read chapter 3 Shannon and Louise are going to try to do some research into the construct validity of the test.

Note. All names on this sample are pseudonyms.

Orientation to Tool 29: Meeting/Conversation Record

Alexa Pearson developed the following tool for documenting meetings with teachers. I have found it very useful in recording the critical elements of an interaction with a group. The following example represents the notes from a meeting with a group of subject area teachers. One of the things that I like about this form is that it has a place for recording "next steps," thus is serves as an action plan, feeding into the next meeting. Tools that set in place or capture cyclical events in the professional learning lives of a school can set in motion recurring actions that can shape the culture of a school in powerful ways.

As I mentioned earlier, literacy coaches are balancing the need to document their work for accountability purposes with the danger of this documentation eating up all of their time. This basic record can help record the heart of a meeting with teachers without claiming excess time. Such forms are potentially the anecdotal records of our conversations with teachers, much like the simple notes we ask teachers to keep as a record of their conference work with children in writers' workshop. Again, in addition to their merit in terms of accountability, they have value historically as you analyze the patterns of work that emerge in your interactions with various teams of teachers.

MEETING/CONVERSATION RECORD

Date _____ Starting time _____ Ending time _____

Participants	
Focus	
Outcomes	
Next steps	
Questions/ concerns to keep working on (focus of next meeting)	
Next meeting date	

Created by Alexa Pearson.

Practical Literacy Coaching: A Collection of Tools to Support Your Work by Jan Miller Burkins.
© 2009 International Reading Association. May be copied for classroom use.

MEETING/CONVERSATION RECORD SAMPLE

Date _11-15-07_   Starting time _1:15_   Ending time _2:50_

Participants	Language arts teacher
Focus	• Freshman lesson planning and essential learnings • How to teach summary • Figure out what mechanics to focus on and how to go about teaching them • How do you assess if students are using reading strategies?

Outcomes	• Lesson plan for next class created
	• Minilesson on oxymoron
	• Pretest (formative assessment) on summary of part two of <u>Speak</u>
	• Brainstormed what to look for in a summary
	   o Book title and author
	   o Chapter title if appropriate
	   o Chronological order of main events
	   o Characters names are included
	   o Conclusion (captures main idea)
	   o No opinion
	• Created a list of mechanics to focus on for summary
	   o Sentence structure (fluency)
	   o Transitions
	   o Present tense
	   o Capitalization
	   o Punctuation for titles
	   o How to avoid using <u>I</u> or <u>you</u>/first or second person
	• Goal = Before holiday break, students will have written two formal summaries
	• Wrote prereading strategy for "Most Dangerous Game"

Next steps	• Pull out the main events from second section of <u>Speak</u> • Create grading ticket for posters (prereading) • Possibly create a good sample/bad sample of poster (using <u>Speak</u>) • Create PowerPoint for lesson plan • Grade summaries and find pieces to use as samples in the minilessons • Alexa will gather "Dangerous Game" resources for teacher.
Questions/ concerns to keep working on (focus of next meeting)	• How to honor the imaginative and creative side of writing. How do you structure a writer's workshop? Can you do this without dropping everything else? • How do you continue to support students' independent reading for SSR? How much monitoring needs to happen here?
Next meeting date	Monday, Nov. 19th at 8:45

Orientation to Tool 30: Literacy Coach's Activity Record

Most literacy coaches I know have to document, in one manner or another, how they spend their time each day. I have to maintain an electronic calendar that is open to my school and district administrators to view any time. I also have to submit monthly hard copies of this calendar, along with other documentation of my time on the job.

Certainly, it is critical that literacy coaches maintain transparency in their work. While an administrator may not ask a literacy coach to document his or her schedule, it is important that the literacy coach take the initiative in record keeping. Even if you have no requirements of this kind, I strongly suggest that you begin completing, of your own initiative, some kind of time log and submitting it to your administration.

Given the novelty of our positions, we must anticipate finding ourselves in the position of defending our work. Literacy coaching is misunderstood and when budgets must be cut, the role of the literacy coach is likely to be scrutinized by school- and district-level administrations.

I recommend using this or some other system of recording your distributions of time. You can complete one of these each week with minimal time commitment and then assemble them electronically or in a binder. For me, if I just keep a very general log of my day, then I can transfer it later into my electronic calendar.

You will notice that the log that follows is not a minute-by-minute account of the literacy coach's day. It is more realistic and is simply a place to record the meat of the coaching work. Incidentally, I usually label my preparation for various events with the same code as the actual event. For example, if I spend 30 minutes in preparation for a demonstration lesson, I will label it "Demonstration Lesson" in my log, or if I spend time preparing for a pre- or postobservation conference, I will label the time as "Teacher Conference." As with any of the tools in this book, you can use the codes I created as a starting point and add to them and revise them to suit your needs.

LITERACY COACH'S ACTIVITY RECORD

Coach _____   Week of _____

Monday

Time	Teacher	Grade	Focus	Code

Tuesday

Time	Teacher	Grade	Focus	Code

Wednesday

Time	Teacher	Grade	Focus	Code

Thursday

Time	Teacher	Grade	Focus	Code

Friday

Time	Teacher	Grade	Focus	Code

Code: Demonstration Lesson (DL); Coteaching (CT); Classroom Visit (CV); Study Group (SG); Teacher Conference (TC); Team Meeting (TM); Other Meeting (OM)

LITERACY COACH'S ACTIVITY RECORD
SAMPLE

Coach _____Burkins_____ Week of _____October 7-11_____

Monday

Time	Teacher	Grade	Focus	Code
8:30–9:30	Reynolds	K	Guided reading	DL
9:30–10:15	Jefferson	5	Literature circles	DL
10:15–11:00	Kimble	2	Assessment	DL
12:00–12:30	Kimble	2	Assessment	TC
1:30–2:00	Reynolds	K	Guided reading	TC
2:00–2:30	Jefferson	5	Literature circles	TC

Tuesday

Time	Teacher	Grade	Focus	Code
8:30–9:30	Smith	K	Guided reading	CV
10:00–11:00	Jones	4	Writer's workshop	CV
11:00–11:30	Team	3	Conferencing	SG
1:00–1:30	Smith	K	Guided reading	TC
1:30–2:15	Echols	1	Interactive writing	CV
2:15–3:00	Team	2	Standards	TM

Wednesday

Time	Teacher	Grade	Focus	Code
8:30–9:30	Lincoln	4	Guided Reading	CV
9:00–10:00	Team	4	Standards	TM
10:00–10:30	Elliott	K	Writer's Workshop	CV
11:00–11:30	Kimball	Admin.	Professional Learning	OM
12:00–12:30	Lincoln	4	Guided Reading	TC
1:00–2:00	Parapros	All	Management	SG

Thursday

Time	Teacher	Grade	Focus	Code
7:30–8:00	Elliott	K	Writer's Workshop	TC
8:00–8:45	Team	1	Writing Samples	TM
9:30–10:15	Vincent	5	Literature Circles	CV
10:30–11:30	Edwards	5	Writer's Workshop	CV
12:30–1:15	Team	K	Writing Samples	TM
1:30–2:30	Vincent	5	Literature Circles	Tc

Friday

Time	Teacher	Grade	Focus	Code
8:15–9:00	Grant	1	Reading Assessments	TC
9:15–10:00	Jefferson	Admin.	RTI	OM
10:00–10:45	Elliott	K	Writer's Workshop	CT
11:30–12:00	Team	5	Writing Assessment	TM
12:30–1:30	Preston	4	Guided Reading	CV
1:30–2:30	Edwards	5	Literature Circles	TC

Code: Demonstration Lesson (DL); Coteaching (CT); Classroom Visit (CV); Study Group (SG); Teacher Conference (TC); Team Meeting (TM); Other Meeting (OM)

Orientation to Tool 31: Grade-Level Notes Form

The value of this form is inversely related to its complexity. This basic tool has really helped me keep track of various communications with teachers. I use it in a number of different ways, and at any given time, I usually have several of these on my desk.

I use them to help me plan or organize topics of discussion by grade level. For example, we have day-long professional learning three times per year where we have substitute teachers relieve a grade-level each day for six days. This means that I get to spend a full day with a single grade-level team of teachers each time. This is a luxurious professional learning opportunity but it is fraught with planning pitfalls. Even from the earliest days of planning, if I begin to jot my ideas down on the Grade-Level Notes Form, I manage to keep my thoughts organized. Planning 50 hours of professional learning in a month and differentiating for the needs of grade-level teams can be overwhelming. This form has been tremendously helpful for me.

I also use this tool to keep track of where I am with grade-level meetings that occur weekly when we don't have our day-long professional learning. If I use this form, I can record thoughts and details as they arise, and they are organized for our meetings. I sometimes even take this form into meetings with me when I meet with each grade-level team during their planning time. I use it to make notes by grade level of things with which I need to follow up.

Finally, I have used this form as I have used the Teacher Checklist (Tool 27), when I need responses or information from grade-level teams rather than from individual teachers. Obviously, this tool is quite versatile; my hope is that you will be able to find even more ways to use it to make your work and communications with grade-level teams easier to manage.

GRADE-LEVEL NOTES FORM

Date _____ Subject _____

Kindergarten
First grade
Second grade
Third grade
Fourth grade
Fifth grade
All

Practical Literacy Coaching: A Collection of Tools to Support Your Work by Jan Miller Burkins.
© 2009 International Reading Association. May be copied for classroom use.

GRADE-LEVEL NOTES FORM SAMPLE

Date *January 6, 2009*   Subject *Notes for February daylong professional learning*

Kindergarten
- *Changes in report card format*
- *Summary of oral language data*
- *Read-aloud format*
- *Reviewing running records*

First grade
- *Guided reading article jigsaw*
- *Strategies for organizing word work*
- *Distributing new LA materials*

Second grade
- *Guided reading article jigsaw*
- *Strategies for organizing word work*
- *Distributing new LA materials*
- *Interpreting running records*

Third grade
- *Examining student writing using state rubrics*
- *Preparing for state writing test*
- *Distributing new LA materials*

Fourth grade
- *Examining student writing using state rubrics*
- *Distributing new LA materials*
- *Vocabulary instructional strategies*

Fifth grade
- *Examining student writing using state rubrics*
- *Preparing for state writing test*
- *Distributing new LA materials*

All
- *Entering literacy data in district spreadsheet*
- *Looking at standards and pacing guide for upcoming quarter*

Coaching Story: Play Fast

With all the demands placed on educators, many of us work in environments where our stress levels are perpetually high. That is, we deal with situations to which our bodies react as if there is an emergency. However, the day-to-day realities of our coaching work are rarely emergencies, at least not the kind that require our "fight or flight" responses to kick in.

This was illustrated to me profoundly in some work I was doing with a second-grade teacher. He was demonstrating a word sorting activity to a pair of children. He was hurrying because he wanted to make sure there was time for me to demonstrate guided reading with two groups before lunch and he was already behind schedule. So he demonstrated the word sorting activity very quickly, with one of his students pretending to be his partner.

The activity was a cooperative one, but because the teacher had demonstrated it in such a rushed way the children perceived that the hurried pace was part of the work. They interpreted his haste to mean that the task was actually competitive. We later looked around the room and observed that all the children were frantically sorting words and pronouncing "winners."

After the lessons, he and I reflected together. He had noticed the way that his behavior had confused his children. He commented that he is constantly at odds with the clock and usually feels like he is behind. He said that the other day he had taken his students outside for recess; they were late and he directed them, "Play fast!"

Oftentimes my task as a literacy coach is to filter the messages that teachers are getting from various school and district administrations. Education in the era of high-stakes and high accountability is, at least to some extent, built on a culture of fear. Furthermore, many times, the expectations of school districts and states are literally impossible to execute, particularly if you consider them as part of an overwhelming assemblage of responsibilities. I work with teachers to help them prioritize the demands on their time and to help them keep some perspective in terms of "fitting it all in."

Coaching Connection: Machines That Make the Work Harder

One evening as I sat in the living room working on this book, I was periodically interrupted by the sounds of my son Christopher crashing and banging around in his bedroom upstairs. I suspected that he was working on a project that was destroying the entire upstairs. (At times like this, the mother I think I am supposed to be collides with the mother I really am. My constructivist philosophy and the practical realities of caring for lots of children and lots of square footage are often in conflict.)

After a couple of hours of banging around, he asked me to come up to his room and see his creation. His room was a cobweb of yarn that spilled into the hallway. Using a shoe, a coat hanger, a chair, and such, he had rigged a chain reaction that would flip on the lights. After a couple of resets and demonstrations, I dutifully applauded his creativity and his inventiveness. He paused and said, "Thanks, but I guess it is one of those machines that really makes things harder. It's probably just easier to flip on the lights."

I couldn't help but wonder, How many procedures, tools, forms, checklists, and so forth do we have in education that actually make our work harder? I often find myself learning some required "tool" that documents in a cumbersome way the work I began doing long before anyone asked me to record it. It is my intention to make your workload lighter and your efforts more productive with this resource. However, if you find that in using one of these tools you are navigating your way through a machine that is making your work harder, please reinvent it to meet your needs.

Resources for Documenting Your Work and Managing Your Time

1. *Why Zebras Don't Get Ulcers* is an acclaimed guide to managing stress. Author Robert M. Sapolsky (2004) offers cutting-edge research and lots of humor along with practical advice as he explains the ways stress comes to bear on our work and our health. He also offers ideas on how to manage our responses to stress.

2. *A Whole New Mind: Why Right-Brainers Will Rule the Future* by Daniel Pink (2006) offers suggestions for mastering your mind—both sides of it. His book is an engaging, provocative read, which is directly relevant to increasing your efficiency at work and to taking care of yourself.

Taking Chapter 6 Personally: How Do *You* Document Your Work and Manage Your Time?

Questions for Reflection

• How are you negotiating the tension between documenting your work and managing your time?

- What are the most important elements of your work, and why? How are you documenting them? How are you sharing this documentation with your administrators?

Possible Action Steps

- Make a list of all the ways you document your work. Think beyond formal record keeping and consider items such as your daily to-do list, teacher checklists, and professional learning agendas.

- Set up a file for keeping any unsolicited, positive feedback you get from teachers. For example, if a teacher writes you a thank-you note for helping organize her classroom library or if a teacher sends you an e-mail telling you how much he appreciated a demonstration lesson, save these. Organize them in a running file. These are powerful documentations of your work.

- Set in place at least one renewing ritual at work to help you manage your energy resources. This might be stretching, stopping and filling your lungs up with air, or listening to some music. Place a tangible representation, such as a picture or object, in your work area to remind you to practice this ritual daily. Identify a physiological prompt or a time of the day to engage in this ritual. Document for a month your practice by simply keeping a tally of how often you practice your ritual. By the time the month is over, you will have developed a new habit for renewing yourself. Then you can begin the process again with another ritual.

- Start keeping a reflective journal of your work. If you do this over time, you will be surprised by the patterns that emerge, and you will learn from yourself. If you don't have time to write in your journal daily, then write in your journal weekly or even monthly.

REFERENCES

Allen, D., & Blythe, T. (2004). *The facilitator's book of questions: Tools for looking together at student and teacher work*. New York: Teachers College Press.

Allen, J. (2006). *Becoming a literacy leader: Supporting learning and change*. Portland, ME: Stenhouse.

Ardalan, D.I. (Producer). (2008, September 14). *Accomplishing big things in small pieces* [Radio magazine]. Washington, DC: National Public Radio.

Blythe, T., Allen, D., & Powell, B.S. (2008). *Looking together at student work* (2nd ed.). New York: Teachers College Press.

Burkins, J.M. (2007). *Coaching for balance: How to meet the challenges of literacy coaching*. Newark, DE: International Reading Association.

Burkins, J.M., & Ritchie, S. (2007). Coaches coaching coaches. *Journal of Language and Literacy Education, 3*(1), 32–47. Retrieved February 25, 2009, from www.coe.uga.edu/jolle/2007_1/coaches.pdf

Calkins, L. (1994). *The art of teaching writing* (2nd ed.). Portsmouth, NH: Heinemann.

Cisneros, S. (1991). *Woman Hollering Creek and other stories*. New York: Random House.

Crane, T.G. (2002). *The heart of coaching: Using transformational coaching to create a high-performance culture*. San Diego, CA: FTA Press.

Curtis, C.P. (2007). *Elijah of Buxton*. New York: Scholastic.

Dozier, C. (2006). *Responsive literacy coaching: Tools for creating and sustaining purposeful change*. Portland, ME: Stenhouse.

Duncan, M. (2006). *Literacy coaching: Developing effective teachers through instructional dialogue*. Katonah, NY: Richard C. Owen.

Eaker, R., DuFour, R., & DuFour, R. (2002). *Getting started: Reculturing schools to become professional learning communities*. Bloomington, IN: Solution Tree.

Goldhammer, R. (1969). *Clinical supervision: Special methods for the supervision of teachers*. New York: Holt, Rinehart and Winston.

Greene, M. (1995). *Releasing the imagination: Essays on education, the arts, and social change*. San Francisco: Jossey-Bass.

Hernandez, N. (2007, June 21). Teacher turnover costs systems millions, study projects. *Washington Post,* B6. Retrieved February 25, 2009, from www.washingtonpost.com/wp-dyn/content/article/2007/06/20/AR2007062002300.html

Hindley, J. (1998). *Inside reading and writing workshops* [Video]. Portland, ME: Stenhouse.

Hough, H.J., Bryk, A., Pinnell, G.S., Kerbow, D., Fountas, I., & Scharer, P. (2008). *Measuring change in the practice of teachers engaged in literacy collaborative professional development: Preliminary results from a four year study*. Paper presented at the 2008 conference of the American Educational Research Association. Retrieved November 3, 2008, from www.literacycoachingonline.org/forums/study-1/measuring-change-in-the-practice-of.attachment/attachment/AERA08_LC_Teacher_Change.pdf

International Reading Association. (2004). *Standards for reading professionals*. Newark, DE: Author. Retrieved September 9, 2008, from www.reading.org/resources/issues/reports/professional_standards.html

Jay, A.B., & Strong, M.W. (2008). *A guide to literacy coaching: Helping teachers increase student achievement*. Thousand Oaks, CA: Corwin.

Johnson-Lambert, D. (2008). *Marching to the beat of a different drummer: A case study of Hartman County School District: Four schools, three literacy coaches, and 160 teachers*. Unpublished manuscript.

Johnston, P.H. (2004). *Choice words: How our language affects children's learning*. Portland, ME: Stenhouse.

Joyce, B.R., & Showers, B. (2002). *Student achievement through staff development* (3rd ed.). Alexandria, VA: Association for Supervision and Curriculum Development.

Knight, J. (2007). *Instructional coaching: A partnership approach to improving instruction*. Thousand Oaks, CA: Corwin.

Larner, M. (2007). *Tools for leaders: Indispensable graphic organizers, protocols, and planning guidelines for working and learning together*. New York: Scholastic.

Loehr, J., & Schwartz, T. (2003). *The power of full engagement: Managing energy, not time, is the key to high performance and personal renewal*. New York: Free Press.

Lyons, C.A., & Pinnell, G.S. (2001). *Systems for change in literacy education: A guide to professional development*. Portsmouth, NH: Heinemann.

McAndrew, D.A. (2005). *Literacy leadership: Six strategies for peoplework*. Newark, DE: International Reading Association.

McCourt, F. (2005). *Teacher man: A memoir*. New York: Scribner.

McKenna, M.C., & Walpole, S. (2008). *The literacy coaching challenge: Models and methods for grades K–8*. New York: Guilford.

Moran, M.C. (2007). *Differentiated literacy coaching: Scaffolding for student and teacher success*. Alexandria, VA: Association for Supervision and Curriculum Development.

Morrison, R. (Executive Producer). (2008, October 26). *CBS Sunday Morning* [Television broadcast]. Los Angeles: Corporate Broadcasting System.

Mraz, M., Algozzine, B., & Kissel, B. (2009). *The literacy coach's companion: PreK–3*. Thousand Oaks, CA: Corwin; Newark, DE: International Reading Association.

National Writing Project. (2006). *Writing for a change: Boosting literacy and learning through social action*. San Francisco, CA: Jossey-Bass.

Pearson, P.D., & Gallagher, M.C. (1983). The instruction of reading comprehension. *Contemporary Educational Psychology, 8*(3), 317–344. doi:10.1016/0361-476X(83)90019-X

Pennac, D. (1994). *Better than life*. Toronto, ON: Coach House Press.

Pink, D.H. (2006). *A whole new mind: Why right-brainers will rule the future*. New York: Penguin.

Rainville, K.N. (2007). Situated identities, power, and positioning: Inside the practices of three literacy coaches in New Jersey. *Dissertation Abstracts International, 68*(6), (UMI No. 3269108).

Rainville, K.N., & Jones, S. (2008). Situated identities: Power and positioning in the work of a literacy coach. *The Reading Teacher, 61*(6), 440–448. doi:10.1598/RT.61.6.1

Ray, K.W. (1999). *Wondrous words: Writers and writing in the elementary classroom*. Urbana, IL: National Council of Teachers of English.

Robb, L. (2000). *Redefining staff development: A collaborative model for teachers and administrators.* Portsmouth, NH: Heinemann.

Rodgers, A., & Rodgers, E.M. (2007). *The effective literacy coach: Using inquiry to support teaching and learning.* New York: Teachers College Press.

Sandvold, A., & Baxter, M. (2008). *The fundamentals of literacy coaching.* Alexandria, VA: Association for Supervision and Curriculum Development.

Sapolsky, R.M. (2004). *Why zebras don't get ulcers* (3rd ed.). New York: Owl Books.

Schmoker, M. (2006). *Results now: How we can achieve unprecedented improvements in teaching and learning.* Alexandria, VA: Association for Supervision and Curriculum Development.

Scott, S. (2002). *Fierce conversations: Achieving success at work and in life, one conversation at a time.* New York: Viking.

Spinelli, J. (2002). *Loser.* New York: Harper Collins.

Strand, M., & Boland, E. (2000). *The making of a poem: A Norton anthology of poetic forms.* New York: W.W. Norton.

Toll, C.A. (2005). *The literacy coach's survival guide: Essential questions and practical answers.* Newark, DE: International Reading Association.

Toll, C.A. (2008). *Surviving but not yet thriving: Essential questions and practical answers for experienced literacy coaches.* Newark, DE: International Reading Association.

Vygotsky, L.S. (1986). *Thought and language* (A. Kozulin, Trans.). Cambridge, MA: MIT Press. (Original work published 1934)

Webb, P.T. (2001). Reflection and reflective teaching: Ways to improve pedagogy or ways to remain racist? *Race, Ethnicity and Education, 4*(3), 245–252. doi:10.1080/13613320120073567

White, B. (1993). *Mama makes up her mind and other dangers of Southern living.* Reading, MA: Addison-Wesley.

INDEX

Note. Page numbers followed by *f* and *t* indicate figures and tables, respectively.